THE SULTAN'S ISTANBUL
ON 5 KURUSH A DAY

Charles FitzRoy

THE SULTAN'S ISTANBUL
ON 5 KURUSH
A DAY

92 illustrations, 18 in color

Thames & Hudson

CONTENTS

I · INTRODUCTION

It seems to me that while other cities may be mortal, this one will remain as long as there are men on earth.

PETRUS GYLLIUS, *THE ANTIQUITIES OF CONSTANTINOPLE*, 1561

There is no part of the Mediterranean more favoured for its situation than the fair city of Istanbul. Surrounded on all sides by water, and overlooking the mighty Bosphorus, which cleaves a path between the continents of Europe and Asia, the city enjoys an unrivalled position.

The splendour of the Istanbul skyline. The city's great mosques lie across the Golden Horn, while the European areas of Galata and Pera are in the foreground.

Venerated since antiquity, when Byzas founded a settlement here on the advice of the oracle in Delphi, in the 4th century AD the city of Byzantium was chosen by the emperor Constantine as his new capital. His successors constructed magnificent palaces and churches, notably the majestic basilica of Ayasofya (Hagia Sophia), which became the envy of all Europe. Safe behind the city's formidable fortifications, the Byzantine emperors reigned over an empire that lasted 1,000 years. The Ottoman sultans, who have ruled here since Mehmet captured the city in 1453 and renamed it Istanbul, have continued to embellish their imperial capital, adorning Topkapi Sarayi, their favourite palace, with a series of

pavilions where they enjoy the pleasures of their harem, and erecting splendid mosques, colleges and baths all over the city.

To reach Istanbul requires a long journey, passing through the plains of the Balkans, or sailing across the Aegean. The route by sea is by far the more enjoyable, though the crew may like to add a frisson of excitement by describing how in former days pirates would emerge from their North African lairs, seize Christian ships and bear away their luckless captives into a life of slavery. This will serve to stimulate your imagination, no doubt already awash with tales of life in the streets of Istanbul: how you can buy anything your heart desires in the teeming bazaars, from a diamond worth a king's ransom to a beautiful black slave girl from Abyssinia, and how the most powerful men in the city are eunuchs who guard the sultan's concubines. As you read this book, you will discover that many of these stories are true, at least in part – and you will learn how to barter in the shops and markets, the secrets of the forbidden area of the harem, where to observe the whirling dervishes transporting themselves into a state of ecstasy and how you can partake of the strange custom of bathing.

With these images crowding your mind, your ship will round a headland and there will before you unfold the unforgettable array of domes and minarets lining the city's skyline. This year of our Lord 1750 is a wonderful time to visit Istanbul. The sultan Mahmud I is an ardent builder, and has done much to increase the splendour of his capital, erecting a series of mosques, schools, libraries and delightful fountains. No wonder Lady Mary Wortley Montagu, wife of the British ambassador, was moved to declare, just a generation ago, how the view from her house encompassed 'the port, the city, the seraglio, and the distant hills of Asia;

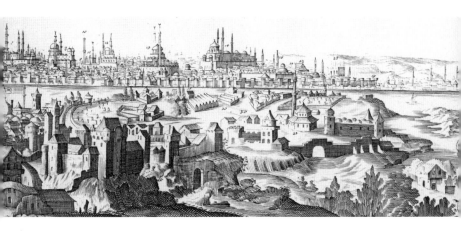

perhaps, all together, the most beautiful prospect in the world'.

As the ship approaches the waterside and you prepare to disembark, you may wonder on the reception you will receive. The more prudent traveller may be armed with a letter from his or her country's ambassador, but you are unlikely to have any problem with the authorities, especially as you will have already passed the frontiers of the Ottoman Empire days if not weeks ago (the empire stretches from the Danube to Persia and from the Crimea to Algiers). Whether you are involved in trade or diplomacy, or perhaps because you are an adventurous soul, you should head for Galata and Pera, on the north side of the Golden Horn, where all Europeans reside.

TURKISH MONEY AND BAKSHISH

A complex subject but one that it is vital you understand.

The most important coin is the *kurush*, a silver coin that will be accepted wherever you go – once valued at approximately equal to the French *ecu* but now worth considerably less.

It is divided into 40 *paras*, each of 3 *akche* – don't bother with akches, they are of little value.

You will need paras for small transactions, kurush for bigger ones.

Remember that, wherever you go, a 'gift' of some money, known as *bakshish* to the locals, should solve the problem – a failure to do so will mean that you get very little done.

Be on your guard against counterfeit coins, which exist in large numbers in Istanbul (see Chapter 4).

Once you have found a suitable lodging, you will need to acquire the help of a good dragoman, or interpreter. Your first port of call should be your country's embassy, where the staff will advise on hiring a suitable one, probably a Phanariot Greek (from the suburb of Phanar). A good dragoman will be the key to the success of your visit. He will be a man of many parts,

The splendidly dressed French ambassador with his dragoman.

The grand mosque of Ayasofya was originally built as a church by the Byzantine emperors.

helping you to cope with the language, which bears no relation to those you will have heard spoken in Europe, explaining the value of the Turkish coinage, and the habit of giving *bakshish*, something that is essential to everyday life in the city. Through him, you will be able to converse with the locals so that you can learn how life is carried on: the way that they eat without cutlery, what clothes women wear when they are at home, what are the most enjoyable festivals, and what is the favourite subject for gossip in the coffee houses?

A good dragoman will also help to keep you out of trouble and, for example, instruct you in how to behave when you visit a mosque. He will also show you how to avoid the janissaries, famous for their arrogance as they swagger down the streets of the city. Their behaviour

Created by nature to be capital of the world.

OGIER GHISELIN DE BUSBECQ,
AMBASSADOR OF THE
HOLY ROMAN EMPIRE, 1550S

may remind you that within living memory they were leading the Turkish hordes to the gates of Vienna. You will learn how essential it is not to anger the authorities; just a generation ago the Venetian ambassador, a hugely important figure, was locked up at the whim of the sultan. Not everyone has been lucky in their choice of dragoman, as you will doubtless hear. For instance Sir James Porter, not long ago, had his interpreter followed, fearing that the urgent message he was carrying would go astray, only to find that he had met up with other dragomen in a house 'where they passed the day very agreeably at cards and other diversions'. But don't worry, you will find much useful advice on the subject of dragomen else-where in this book.

There is plenty of other useful infor-mation to learn. This is a Muslim state and you should always remember that Christians are very much second-class citizens. Turkish dates are based on the flight of the Prophet Mohammed from Mecca to Medina on 15 July AD 622, as your dragoman will explain, and the calendar is lunar, with 12 months, each 29 or 30 days long. As the total is only 354 days, rather than 365, this means that festivals and anniversaries change from year to year – which can be confusing. The climate in Istanbul is normally very clement and conducive to good health, although this is some-what dependent on the direction of the wind. In summer the south wind can occasionally bring the scalding heat of the deserts of Africa while in winter the wind from the north can carry with it the bleak chill of the Russian steppes.

If you want to read up on the city's history before you arrive, the stand-ard work, which seems to have been translated into all the main European languages, is Dimitrie Cantemir's *History of the Turks*. Cantemir himself had a highly adventurous life; born in Moldavia he moved to Istanbul, where he lived for many years, before defect-ing to Russia. When Peter the Great was defeated by the Turks, Cantemir was terrified of the retribution that the Turks would carry out for his defec-tion, and escaped by hiding in the Tsar's coach.

A SHORT HISTORY OF ISTANBUL

Traditionally founded by Byzas in 660 BC, the city lies on an excellent defensive site between the Sea of Marmara and the Golden Horn, overlooking the Bosphorus.

The city of Byzantium benefited greatly from all the land-borne trade between Europe and Asia, and from shipping going up the Bosphorus to the Black Sea.

In a ceremony in the Hippodrome on 11 May 330, the emperor Constantine declared the city the new capital of the Roman Empire.

The city was renamed Constantinople, with the newly established Christianity as its religion and Greek as its language.

For 1,000 years the Byzantine Empire remained the greatest and richest power in the Mediterranean world.

In 1453, after a six-week siege, the army of the Ottoman Turks led by Mehmet II (later 'the Conqueror') stormed and took the city.

During the 16th century, under Suleyman the Magnificent, the Ottoman Empire was the greatest in the world – and Suleyman's architect Sinan built many of the most beautiful mosques in the city.

Since the failure of the siege of Vienna in 1683, the Ottoman Empire has been in decline, but the present sultan Mahmud I and his predecessor Ahmed III have continued to beautify the city with new buildings and fountains.

II · A DESCRIPTION
OF THE CITY

The unexampled Beauties of the Prospect she affords, are such as render her the Seat of Pleasure, and the Paradise of Nature.

AARON HILL, *A FULL AND JUST ACCOUNT OF THE PRESENT STATE OF THE OTTOMAN EMPIRE*, 1710

Your initial impression on arriving in Istanbul is likely to be how very different life is from anything you have experienced before. Although it is easy enough to find accommodation in the areas of Galata and Pera, to the north of the Golden Horn, where all Europeans live, there is so much else that is totally alien. For a start, there is no question of you wandering freely through the city. Your lodgings will be staffed by Turkish servants, probably including janissaries (see Chapter 5), one of whom will always be available to accompany you when you venture out, and you will also have your dragoman, who will act as an interpreter in your dealings with the locals. They, and many others, will be expected to be rewarded with bakshish, which is such a central feature of Turkish life. As the Marquis de Villeneuve, the French ambassador in the 1720s, commented, he needed to make 'little presents and gratifications which here make an

A bird's-eye view from Uskudar looking across the Bosphorus to Istanbul.

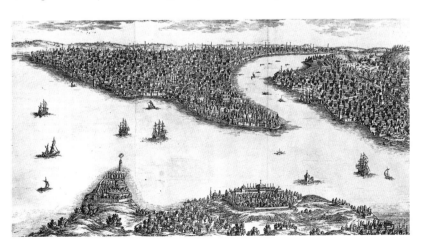

essential part of all intercourse and are expected as Tokens of Respect... when an acquaintance is once made, there is a constant train of little wants'.

You will soon find how dependent you are on your guide. This is not a city where you can walk anywhere, and it is vital that you make friends with him so he can show you the bazaars and help you to negotiate a deal should you wish to make a purchase. If you wish to visit the great mosques, which are such a wonderful ornament to the city, you will also need your guide to organize a visit since, in theory, they are off limits to non-Muslims. In the rougher areas of the city he will also protect you; it has been known for foreigners to be insulted, or even, on rare occasions, to be stoned by the locals.

One aspect of the city of Istanbul that you will discover quickly is how very different the various areas are. Each district is centred on a religious building and the distinctive architecture of the mosque, church or synagogue will tell you whether you are in a Muslim, Christian or Jewish neighbourhood. In addition, you will learn to recognize the way that, although all streets are unpaved and seem equally dusty in summer, or muddy in winter, the ones in Turkish suburbs are wider and cleaner than those in areas inhabited by Greeks, Armenians and Jews. Turkish streets are also more often filled with the scent of flowers, roses and tulips, since Turkish women, who spend so much time at home, decorate the exterior of their houses with attractive window boxes overflowing with carnations, roses and geraniums.

Although the sounds emanating from every neighbourhood are similar – the cry of hawkers selling their wares, the shouts of porters making their way through the crowded streets,

The harbour of Constantinople is the most spacious, the finest, and the most advantageously situated in the World, it being the rendezvous of two Seas; and whatever Wind blows, one may see at all times Vessels sailing into and out, both of one and the other.

AUBRY DE LA MOTRAYE,

TRAVELS THROUGH EUROPE, ASIA AND INTO PARTS OF AFRICA, 1730

The Orient has been an enduring subject for western artists: here, Jean-Étienne Liotard depicts a French lady with her veiled slave.

the soothing clack of backgammon counters in the cafes, and the growls of dogs scrapping over morsels of food – in Muslim ones you will soon recognize the call to prayer from the local mosque.

You will also learn before long that some neighbourhoods have a very distinctive smell. Most notorious of all is Yedikule, home to the fortress of the same name (commonly known as the Castle of the Seven Towers), next to the majestic Land Walls near the Sea of Marmara, where the smell is quite repellent. This is where the tanneries are located, and the whole area is impregnated with the stench of decaying carcasses, mixed with urine and leather. The tanners appear quite immune to the execrable sight and smell of the piles of fleeces and skins, and carry on their work, stripped to the waist, their torsos mottled with blood. There are hordes of scavenging dogs searching for scraps among the heaps of discarded waste. No wonder few outsiders venture here, and the authorities steer clear of the area too – which is why it is rumoured to harbour thieves and murderers fleeing justice.

GALATA AND PERA

An agreeable mixture of gardens, pine and cypress trees, palaces, mosques and public buildings, raised one above the other.

LADY WORTLEY MONTAGU,
LETTERS FROM THE LEVANT, 1716–18

North of the Golden Horn, the suburbs of Galata and Pera, where you will be staying, have been a home for Europeans for centuries, ever since

Many beautiful drinking fountains have been erected around the city in recent years; this one is in Pera.

the Genoese and Venetians had their main trading bases here in Byzantine times. It was a self-contained enclave away from the centre of government (Pera is also known as Beyoglu, named after Bailo, the title of the Venetian ambassador, whose palace is one of the grandest buildings in the district). It is the one area where the Ottoman government permits infidels to build houses, and that is why foreign embassies are based here. You will soon get to know the district, filled with tempting shops and noisy taverns catering for sailors who come up from the waterside at Tophane. Since Muslims are forbidden from drinking, at least in public, these taverns are the best places in town to buy alcohol. If you wander through Galata and Pera at night you will also recognise the sight of the nightwatchmen who patrol the streets, ready to arrest those whose drunken behaviour leads them into fights.

THE SEVEN HILLS
AND THE GOLDEN HORN

Before starting to explore the city, you can gain a good overall impression from your base in Galata or Pera. The Golden Horn lies at your feet; it takes its romantic name from the glorious colour of the water at sunset. It is one of the great natural harbours of the world, an inlet of the Bosphorus shaped like a horn or, more appropriately one might imagine, like a scimitar, and stretching inland for some 4 miles. There was once a great chain defending its mouth, a barrier that defied even the mighty Mehmet the Conqueror in 1453, though the sultan, not to be deterred, commanded his battle-hardened soldiers to drag his ships over the hill of Galata to reach the Horn. Half a century later, Leonardo da Vinci, the most brilliant artist and scientific inventor in Italy, was commissioned by Beyazit II to produce a 700-foot, single-span bridge over the water – but, like so many of Leonardo's brilliant designs, this astoundingly ambitious scheme was never executed.

Across the Golden Horn rise the seven hills of old Istanbul. The Byzantines, who saw themselves as the heirs of the ancient Romans, attached great symbolism to the fact that Constantinople, like Rome, was built on seven hills. Arrayed before you are the magnificent silhouettes of a series of domes and minarets. The original city was founded on the easternmost hill, an incomparable setting surrounded by the Golden Horn to the north, the Bosphorus to the east and the Sea of Marmara to the south. It contains many of the most important monuments of Istanbul: Topkapi Sarayi, Ayasofya, the Blue Mosque and the Hippodrome (all described in Chapter 6), as well as exotic-sounding streets such as the Bushy Beard, Sweating Whiskers, Ibrahim of Black Hell, and the Avenue of the White Moustache.

The second hill is of equal interest. It is the commercial centre of the

city, overflowing with the shops and markets that are such an attractive feature of Istanbul. Further west the third hill is dominated by the splendid complex of buildings surrounding the Suleymaniye (the great mosque of Suleyman the Magnificent). The majestic Roman Aqueduct of Valens links the third and fourth hills. The mosque of Mehmet the Conqueror, known as the Fatih Mosque, and that of Selim the Grim, crown the fourth and fifth hills. Beyond you can glimpse the minarets of the Mihrimah Mosque on the sixth hill, built by the favourite daughter of Suleyman.

If you now want to begin exploring Istanbul on foot, make sure you are

This elaborate fountain outside Topkapi Sarayi was built by Ahmed III.

wearing some tough shoes. The hills are much steeper than they look on first inspection. Crossing the Golden Horn from Galata, you will be met by picturesque markets, with a never-ending fleet of boats unloading fish, fruit and vegetables, a frenetic scene with a cacophony of noise as the vendors sell their wares to a stream of passengers disembarking from boats of every shape and size. From there, and with the help of a guide or your dragoman, you can head off to visit some of the must-see sights described in chapters 6 and 7. If, at any time, you want to take a break, there are numerous cafes in every district to provide a welcome distraction. They are often set in a square dominated by a charming fountain. Inside you will find locals (only men, of course) whiling away their time drinking and playing games while exchanging news and gossip.

If you are feeling more indolent, take a boat up the Golden Horn. You will easily find one for hire on the Galata waterfront. Reclining on comfortable cushions, your oarsmen will set off upstream with practised ease. Almost immediately you will pass, on your right, the hilly suburb of Kasimpasa, overlooking the arsenal of Tersane, an immense naval base consisting of a multitude of dockyards, storehouses for gunpowder and munition factories, enclosed by a high wall. There were once 120 galleys moored here, crewed by captured Christian slaves who spent their lives toiling at the oars. The ships that remain are a truly splendid sight, with their high, carved prows, golden lanterns and crimson standards.

A little further west up the Golden Horn is Haskoy, a crowded suburb inhabited by many Orthodox Jews, both Sephardim (from Spain and Portugal) and Ashkenazi (from Central Europe). On your left, across the water, lies Phanar, named after the Gate of the Lighthouse, known as the Porta Phanarion, and for centuries the Greek centre in Istanbul. Many of the Phanariots, as they are known,

have become very wealthy, and the area is filled with their splendid mansions, built like fortresses with massive walls and iron doors. The Phanariots, although they have retained their religion, have served the Ottoman Empire faithfully and the most successful are princes in their own right, ruling the far-flung provinces of Wallachia and Moldavia on the Danube. Phanariot Greeks traditionally provide dragomen (interpreters) to the government and to foreign embassies, and if you have

OKMEYDAN

Named after the archery field, where the sultans like to test their prowess with the bow and arrow.

It stands on the hillside above the arsenal at Tersane.

You can still see the elegant kiosk from where the archers took aim, and the markers celebrating their most remarkable shots.

This is a favourite spot where locals meet up during festivals – enormous crowds enjoyed a feast here a few years ago to celebrate the circumcision of Ahmed III's sons.

The site also serves as an assembly point in times of plague and earthquake.

In winter, when it snows, the grand vizier hastens here with a task force whose job is to shovel the snow into great pits – it is then used for the important purpose of cooling drinks.

followed the advice in this book you will probably have hired one yourself. The key position is chief dragoman to the Porte (the government, which takes its name from the palace and office of the grand vizier, the Sublime Porte), since this role carries control of the means of communication between senior figures in government, particularly the grand vizier, and foreigners. For the unscrupulous, this gives very good opportunities for accepting bribes or promises of preferment, which has undoubtedly helped the leading dragomen achieve great wealth.

Some of the ancient churches that are scattered throughout this area have fascinating histories, in particular St Mary of the Mongols, named after the illegitimate daughter of a Byzantine emperor. She was sent in the late 13th century to Mongolia to marry the Great Khan of the Mongols and lived happily with him in Persia. When he died, she returned to Constantinople, where she ended up as a nun at this church.

This bank of the Golden Horn testifies to the cosmopolitan and diverse character of Istanbul. To the west of Phanar lies the Jewish suburb of Balat; its name derives from a corruption of 'palation', or palace, since the area was once the site of the Byzantine palace of Blachernae, built next to a famous spring believed since antiquity to possess miraculous powers. Further up the Golden Horn is the neighbourhood of Eyup, a holy place for all Muslims (see Chapter 8). Non-Muslims are not particularly welcome here, so you need to be careful if you decide to visit.

The most beautiful spot on the Golden Horn is the headwaters, known as the Sweet Waters of Europe. Locals flock here during the summer months. It is best to visit at sunset when the view is magnificent. During the last sultan's reign he created a magical place called Sa'adabad, where he would throw extravagant parties in beautiful palaces and gardens. Though much was destroyed with the fall of Ahmed III, enough remains to give you a good idea of Sa'adabad's former splendour.

USKUDAR

They look as rough as lions, and are ready to tear a Frank to pieces.
LORD BALTIMORE ON THE INHABITANTS OF
USKUDAR, *A TOUR TO THE EAST*, 1767

The extensive suburb of Uskudar, the site of the ancient Greek Chrysopolis, stands on the Asian side of the Bosphorus and is well worth a visit. It retains a more rural atmosphere than the centre of the city across the water. The most exciting time to come here is for the monthly arrival of the caravan, composed of hundreds of camels and mules, laden with carpets and rugs, spices and scents, and slaves and gold from the far cities of Persia and Syria. The best place to see it is the Square of the Falconers, where your boat will land. It is even more entertaining to watch the departure of the annual pilgrimage

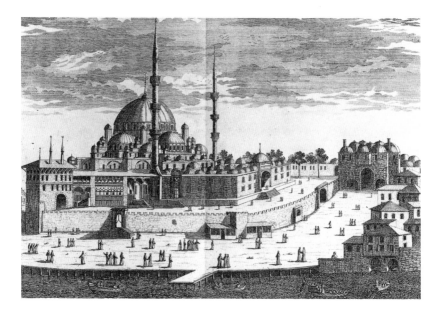

The Yeni Valide Mosque in Uskudar is one of the most impressive buildings erected so far this century.

that leaves from here for Mecca (see Chapter 8). This is a moment of high excitement, and a great crowd gathers to see off the caravan, weeping women embracing their loved ones, holy men praying for the success of the journey, while all around jugglers and acrobats entertain the crowd, and musicians add to the general din.

The prolific architect Sinan erected some of his finest mosques here during the 16th century, notably the splendid Atik Valide Mosque, built for Nurbanu Sultan, an extraordinarily powerful woman and virtual ruler of the Ottoman Empire. The last

sultan, Ahmed III, was very fond of this area, and built several monuments in a flamboyant style strongly influenced by French architecture; there is a lovely fountain off the Square of the Falconers, and nearby is the Yeni Valide Mosque, dedicated to his mother. The Maiden's Tower, standing just 200 yards offshore and serving as a lighthouse, is a romantic memento of the past, named after a princess who was once incarcerated there.

The geographical position of Uskudar makes it popular with the Turks, who feel an affinity with their ancestors from the Anatolian hinterland, and who often choose to be buried in this part of the city. The most popular venue is the vast cemetery of Karaca Ahmet. South of Uskudar, in the Sea of

Marmara, lie the Princes' Islands, once a place of exile for Byzantine emperors and empresses who had lost their thrones; many eminent figures ended their lives gazing wistfully across the water to the city they had once ruled. Although these islands have a feeling of peace compared to the pace of life in the city, there are some secluded locations on them where dissolute locals are reputed to get up to no good.

> [The Turks] go to these [Princes'] Islands, inhabited only by Christian Greeks, with a design to booze it about briskly, and when they get drunk, they commit all the disorders that their inflam'd heads can devise.
>
> GUILLAUME-JOSEPH GRELOT, A LATE VOYAGE TO CONSTANTINOPLE, 1683

THE BOSPHORUS

A boat trip up the Bosphorus is a most enjoyable excursion (see Chapter 9). This narrow strait, 20 miles long, and running from the Black Sea to the Mediterranean, divides Europe from Asia. It is a treacherous piece of water, with very strong currents.

The Bosphorus's rich history is intertwined with myth. 'The Ford of Cows', named after the goddess Io who was turned into a heifer by her lover Zeus to protect her from his wife Hera, has inspired many legends. It was up the Bosphorus that Jason and the Argonauts sailed in search of the fabulous Golden Fleece. It was over this stretch of water that the two Persian emperors Darius and Xerxes watched their vast and seemingly invincible armies march across bridges of boats when they launched their ill-fated invasions of Greece in the 5th century BC. Centuries later Justinian's great general Belisarius, not content with defeating the emperor's enemies on land, fought a whale in the Bosphorus. One thousand years later, Frenchman Petrus Gyllius recounted how he was terrified by his encounter with an enormous shark in the ominous waters.

> The Bosphorus with one key opens and closes two worlds, two seas.
>
> PETRUS GYLLIUS

Although the Bosphorus now seems to present a more peaceful sight, there is a darker side to this beautiful view. Every year boats collide in the treacherous currents. And rumour has it that a lady of the harem who has incurred the wrath of the sultan or one of his chief eunuchs is sewn into a sack and thrown from a boat at night into the swirling waters, her naked body having 'only the blue tissue of the waves of the sea for clothing'.

The best way to explore the Bosphorus is to hire a caique from the mouth of the Golden Horn. These elegant craft, built of polished planks of beechwood, are incredibly swift. Barely have you seated yourself comfortably among the cushions before the narrow boat is

Taking a boat onto the Bosphorus is a most enjoyable excursion.

skimming over the water, darting past the crowd of cutters, barques, skiffs and rafts bringing metals, furs and ice down from the Black Sea, precious alum from the mines of northern Anatolia and silks from Iran. A boat trip on the Bosphorus is also a wonderfully relaxing way to catch glimpses into the elegant *yalis* (waterside residences) lining its banks, filled with precious textiles and ceramics (see Chapter 9).

NATURAL DISASTERS

The three perils in Pera are plague, fire and interpreters.

TRADITIONAL SAYING

Istanbul lies at the centre of an earthquake zone and you will hear frequent tales of their occurrence and the devastation they cause, wrecking whole streets, uprooting trees and causing disastrous floods. In 1509 there was an earthquake of such severity that it lasted for 40 days, resulting in massive destruction. And just five years ago a great rain storm affected the whole city, destroying 200 houses in Kasimpasa. Rain fell from the sky that tasted salty, a phenomenon so strange that it caused 'people with discernment to ask for God's forgiveness'. It has even been known for lightning to strike gunpowder stores, causing huge explosions. The Turks seem very fatalistic about these natural disasters; they believe that if it is the will of Allah, they must accept it with resignation.

They are equally phlegmatic about the weather, which can be very changeable. If you plan to remain in the city during winter, you'll need to wrap up warmly in furs, if you can afford them, because there are sometimes blizzards, and it has even been known for rivers and springs to freeze. If you witness a hailstorm, you may see hailstones 'as large as a man's foot'; they can be so destructive that tiles are torn from roofs, wooden boards fall from houses, and boats on the Bosphorus capsize.

Even more frightening than storms and earthquakes is the plague, which occurs all too frequently, far more often than in Western Europe. The sultan and his family are no more immune than his subjects and, at the first sign of an epidemic, will leave the city. He no doubt remembers only too clearly how nineteen of Murad III's daughters died in a particularly virulent outbreak of 'the angel of death' in 1598. As soon as rumour starts of a new outbreak, people join the sultan by fleeing the city in their thousands. It seems only the Greeks, noted for their medical skills, are willing to treat plague victims. As the French traveller Monsieur de Guys put it, 'The Greek women at Constantinople who attend the sick, never require anything but brandy to keep it off: of which they drink often in the course of the day.'

FIRE

Another common hazard is fire. Some 30 years ago, Lady Wortley Montagu observed that most families had had the misfortune of watching their house burn down once or even twice. She was amazed by the imperturbable way in which Turks coped with this disaster. It

is often caused by the manner in which locals heat their houses. They use a tandoor, a cylindrical, clay oven placed in the ground heated by a pan of charcoal with hot ashes, and a padded quilt thrown over it to keep the heat in. You can imagine how easy it is for fire to break out. As Turkish houses are not designed to keep out the cold, these tandoors are very popular but also very dangerous.

The authorities are all too aware of the danger of fire. You will see watchtowers scattered throughout the city, and night patrols are tasked with looking out for fires and dealing with them. The sultans have issued numerous decrees ordering the inhabitants of Istanbul to use stone, lime and mud for their buildings, rather than the cheaper wood, to decrease the likelihood of fire. Fire can be catastrophic for business and, if you are staying in Galata, you will notice that foreign merchants prefer to build their warehouses in stone.

If you do happen to have the misfortune to be caught up in a fire, it is a terrifying sight, with whole streets devastated, houses crashing to the ground in smouldering ruins, splinters of burning wood scattered to the winds. With the prevalence of wooden houses, the city is like a tinder box. Once the fire has started, the narrowness of the streets increases the danger of it spreading, added to which the wind often changes direction. If it is very strong it has been known for thousands of houses to be burned in a matter of hours. Bakeries and baths, although they are checked every two or three months, are particularly prone to fires. Sometimes a fire breaks out on a ship which drifts in to the shore, setting the surrounding houses ablaze.

When a fire breaks out, a signal is hoisted and a cannon fired, the number of discharges indicating which quarter it is in. A team of young, active, lightly-clad men will immediately set off from the Galata Tower or from the two towers on either side of the mouth of the Golden Horn, whichever is nearer the site of the conflagration. They are armed with axes, long hooked poles, leather buckets and portable pumps, some of the firefighters carrying primitive fire engines that look like small boxes on their shoulders. These are a recent invention of a French engineer who converted to Islam and adopted the name of Gercek Davud. They are under the command of the head firefighter, whose powers include the use of cannon to blow up unsafe houses.

The sultan himself takes a close interest in firefighting. As so often, there is a protocol to follow when one breaks out. One account records this in some detail. As soon as he receives the news, the guard informs the chief eunuch, who goes straight to the sultan's residence. He announces the event to the five maids who keep watch alternately during the night. One of these maids then puts on a red turban (the sign of fire) and enters the sultan's bedchamber. When he awakes, the sultan immediately notices the red turban, demands to know in what quarter is the fire, dresses and hastens with his retinue to the scene of the conflagration.

III · THE LOCALS
AND THEIR CUSTOMS

I live in a place that very well represents the tower of Babel.... My grooms are Arabs; my footmen French, English and Germans; my nurse an Armenian; my steward an Italian; my janissaries Turks.

LADY WORTLEY MONTAGU

Istanbul is a cosmopolitan city; it is extraordinary how many different nationalities you will come across living here. First and foremost come the Turks. You would have thought that your fellow Europeans, especially those who have been living here for years, would have made an effort to understand their hosts. And yet this does not seem to be the case. All agree that the Turks are, as a whole, mild and self-controlled, but most see this as a fault, interpreting their passive demeanour as demonstrating their proud and overbearing nature, or, alternatively, as showing fatalism and indifference. Moreover, this passivity does not fit in with the aggression and ferocity that the Turks have traditionally shown in battle.

As a result, many westerners take a dim view of their hosts. Only last year the British ambassador, whose job it

is to cultivate good relations with the Turks and their government, made the arrogant assumption that it was impossible to find one who was 'unprejudiced and well informed'. Not surprisingly, many Turks take an equally dim view of Europeans, openly referring to them as hogs, infidels and blasphemers. Indeed, the dragomen who accompany Europeans wear special clothes and yellow shoes to prevent locals attacking them. They are known to the Turks

Janissaries love to wear the most exotic costumes and headgear.

as swineherds, and Pera is insultingly referred to as the 'pig quarter'.

The Europeans are generally known to the Turks as Franks, indicating the fact that the French have dominated European trade with the Ottoman Empire for several hundred years, and that the French king had been the closest ally of the sultan. And yet, despite the amount of trade Europeans do with the Turks, they make little effort to learn Turkish, or to attempt to understand their culture or religion.

You will come across many Greeks on the streets of Istanbul, and you will soon learn to recognize them from the open nature of their expressions, and the spontaneity of their gestures. They are lively and entertaining company, with a natural wit, and, when you see two people arguing in the street, the chances are that they are Greeks since they love nothing better than a good argument. They are widely seen as plausible rascals, adept at bartering, their fingers 'as nimble as their genius is sprightly', as the English traveller Sir James Porter commented. Many visitors admire the Greek women, walking with a classical poise, though they have a curious idea of how to dress, appearing in the height of summer in black velvet robes, laden with gold embroidery.

The Armenians are more grave and dignified, tall and light-skinned, often verging on the corpulent. They are less easily identifiable, as they dress like Turks. Like the Greeks they have a reputation for being honest and adept at business, and there is a saying among Europeans that they are born shrewd. They also make the best grooms and love horses, though the Turks are less complimentary, referring to them as the 'camels of empire'.

The Jews are another race well known for their business acumen. Lady Wortley Montagu commented on this, and contrasted it with the general Turkish apathy. She described how the Jews have managed to draw 'the whole trade of the empire into their hands, partly by the firm union among themselves, and partly by the idle temper and want of industry in the Turks.... Even the English, French and Italian merchants, who are sensible of their artifices, are, however, forced to entrust their affairs to their negotiation.'

The lowest class of labourers, always excepting slaves, are the immigrants who pour into Istanbul, poor people from all over the Ottoman Empire coming to seek their fortune. They tend to take up unskilled work, and many of the city's porters and boatmen that you encounter will have recently arrived from the provinces.

CLOTHING

As you wander through the streets, you will be struck by the exotic nature and bewildering variety of people's clothing. The government has tried, on numerous occasions, to persuade its citizens to dress in a less flamboyant

The Sultan's turban carrier plays an important role in the complicated rigmarole of dressing his master.

Tradesmen often don a particular garb, such as the dustmen who wear red leather smocks. Perhaps the most striking garment is the turban, which appears in all shapes and sizes. The chief dragoman to the Porte is the only official to wear a fur turban as a matter of course, but other than that it is a baffling experience trying to distinguish all the different ranks in the Ottoman hierarchy from this important piece of headgear. You will find it much easier to tell races apart by looking at the colour of their trousers and slippers, red and yellow or white for Turks, black for Greeks, purple and violet for Armenians, and sky-blue for Jews.

An Ottoman gentleman wants to look his best when he appears in public. He wears a caftan, which in winter is lined with fur. Beneath he will wear a loose, brightly coloured robe tied with a belt or sash, often holding documents, a money bag or a dagger. Under this robe he has a plain shirt, and under this a cotton vest and underpants tied just below the knee or at the ankle. On his feet the gentleman will wear leather or cloth slippers. If he goes out onto the streets he will put on heavy leather shoes or loose black boots if he is riding.

fashion, but nobody listens. The Turks see their clothes as a way to proclaim their status: the grander the position the richer the clothes. They take their lead from the sultan, the only Turk, along with the grand vizier, to wear gold- and silver-threaded openwork embroidery. His nobles therefore take pride in dressing in the richest materials, including velvet, taffeta, silk, satin, brocade and cotton. Only the sultan wears black fox, incredibly expensive and difficult to obtain, whereas his high-ranking officials content themselves with sable or ermine.

When you see a Turkish woman in the streets, she will be dressed in the *ferace*, a long flowing garment, often of English cloth, which is meant to hide the finer garments beneath, and, of course, the shape of the woman's body. Over her face she wears a *yasmak*, a scarf of fine muslin that covers her face apart from her eyes and nose, and over this a black veil, or *pece*, which has become more transparent in recent years, much to the horror of the government. The authorities regard women as a potential provocation and have made all sorts of rules regarding this garment, with little effect. Muslim women also wear distinctive yellow shoes, unlike non-Muslims, whose shoes are black or dark-coloured.

At home, in contrast to these drab clothes, upper-class Turkish ladies display a dazzling wardrobe, although you are unlikely to have the opportunity to witness this. They wear wide trousers made of fine brocade from Bursa, either of damask or silk and embroidered with flowers, and a long shirt, with wide, pointed sleeves, fastened at the neck with a jewel. In addition, they often wear a waistcoat and a caftan. In winter, like their menfolk, those who can afford it wear furs. On their feet women wear soft kid slippers of Moroccan leather. Not content with this elaborate wardrobe, Turkish women love to cover their clothing with ornaments. Belts are adorned, sometimes with a diamond buckle, diamonds are sewn into nightcaps, and even domestic objects are covered with jewels.

Poorer women, unable to afford such finery, use embroidery instead of jewelry, although some allow themselves the extravagance of a gold coin in their headscarves. Normally, these women wear full trousers and a smock, are likely to go barefoot at home although they will put on slippers and overshoes when they venture out. Aaron Hill, an English traveller to Istanbul at the beginning of the century, wrote scathingly of their attire, noting how the 'meaner sort go Bare Legg'd, with Girdles twisted round their Middles, and a Dirty Towel wrapt about their Heads'.

THE FASCINATION OF TURKISH WOMEN

The fact that Muslim women are covered up when they venture outside the home only increases their allure and they are a source of great fascination among all Europeans, especially men. If you follow a woman down a street, dressed in her ferace and yasmak, with only the eyes visible, you can give your imagination free rein. It may be that you are pursuing a full-bodied matron with large dark eyes and full lips, or a slip of a woman with a slender waist and pure skin. Gossips speculate that a woman's anonymity means that she has endless opportunities to indulge in illicit liaisons. They maintain that a woman embarking on such a liaison will don

Buy me, my lord. Take me, if you think me capable to please you, or if you doubt that I am false or counterfeit money, send me to be proved by the Sheraph [money-changer].

18TH-CENTURY TURKISH LOVE SONG

All westerners are intrigued by Muslim women hidden behind their veils.

a crude ferace of black cloth (normally they are in pink or lilac).

On first appearance, a Turkish woman seems to enjoy a much inferior lifestyle to her western counterpart, compelled to spend most of her life in the home, only permitted to bare her face before her closest male relatives, and with the prospect of sharing her husband with other wives. However, should the marriage prove unsuccessful, the wife is entitled to sue for divorce on the grounds of her husband's cruelty or desertion (it is, of course, far easier for a husband to divorce his wife). In the event of separation or divorce, if the wife decides to return to her family she retains her own property, and can call for the return of her dowry. She also can also keep her sons until the age of seven and her daughters until puberty. If the wife should die, it is her female relatives who take custody of the children.

A married woman also chooses her son's bride, and after her son's marriage the mother remains the dominant figure in the household. The new wife, much to her chagrin, must always wait until her mother-in-law is seated before sitting at the table herself for a meal. She cannot even help herself to food until the older woman has been served.

Although Islam advocates polygamy, you will find, in fact, that most men are monogamous. They simply cannot afford the expense of setting up separate households for each wife. However, this certainly does not mean that Turkish men regard women as their equals. When Lord Charlemont, an Irishman on the Grand Tour, asked his janissary servant whether he could meet his wife, he received an unequivocal reply. The janissary told him, in broken English: 'Ah master! Me fight for you. Me die for you – no force. But my wife not show. No good Turkoman show his wife.' The janissary followed up by declaring: 'My last wife, no good wife. She not wash my shirt. She not make my broth. I sell her – no force. Buy another.' This sums up the difficulty of meeting Turkish women.

LIFE INSIDE ISTANBUL'S HOUSES

As you wander the streets, you will notice that the majority of houses are built of wood, a relatively cheap material. Turks are very adept in their use of wood, and you will see many examples of their fine craftsmanship on your walks through the city. Streets tend to be narrow and crooked, so it is difficult to get an idea of the layout of these houses. They are often of three or even more storeys, the upper ones projecting, giving a zigzag effect. In some places you will see them almost touching one another across the street, so that little natural light reaches ground level, enhancing a feeling of mystery. A glance of a figure through a latticed window, or the murmur of a subdued conversation, will fire your imagination.

If you do obtain access to a Turkish house you will be greeted with the words 'Peace be with you'. You will find that men and women have their own apartments, a segregation that Europeans living in Istanbul have tended to copy. Anyone who can afford it has a garden, since the Turks

MEN'S AND WOMEN'S QUARTERS

There are separate living quarters in Turkish houses for the two sexes, each with its own entrance. The male area is known as the *selamlik*, while the female one is called the *haremlik*.

A *seraglio* is the living quarters of the wives and concubines in an Ottoman household. Also known as a harem, though the word can be used to refer to the women within. Apart from the husband, men are strictly forbidden from entering.

The kitchen is normally opposite the entrance or in the courtyard – cooking is done in a brick oven or over a shallow tray of coal.

Living room furniture tends to be sparse – a few low tables and a low divan round the walls. Rugs and cushions are spread liberally around the rooms; bedding consists of mattresses stuffed with cotton.

Since women spend so much more time in the home than men, their rooms tend to have more furnishings.

Social activity in both the selamlik and haremlik tends to be very formal.

Baskets are very useful for storage; kerchiefs (square cloths, normally of muslin, with an embroidered border) hold clothes and linen.

Many houses have their own baths, which always consist of three apartments. Otherwise, there is a small washing room, with a hole in the floor for water to escape.

Shoes are left outside, as when visiting a mosque.

are passionate about flowers. Their favourites are tulips, for which there was a complete mania a few years ago.

Life is very different for the lower classes. They tend to live in small, cramped houses, set in disorderly fashion along side streets. There is no space to have separate areas for the sexes, so a curtain of thick felt cloth hangs down the middle of the living room to provide a modicum of decorum. This is where the whole family sits, eats, socializes and sleeps together. Apart from a cooking stove there is minimal furniture: just some rugs for bedding which are kept rolled up when not in use, and a prayer mat which is unrolled and aligned towards Mecca when a family member wants to say his or her prayers. A few of these families might have enough money to afford a house with a small interior courtyard, and a room for storage.

KEY CEREMONIES

The birth of a child is a major cause for celebration. After being born, the child is named and dressed with a blue-bead amulet with a red ribbon placed on its shoulder to ward off the Evil Eye. The mother is put to bed with rich shawls and quilts. Friends and relatives soon arrive, bearing gifts; they are invited to help themselves from baskets of sweets, before entering the bedchamber where they greet the smiling mother. The mother goes to the baths 40 days after the birth, accompanied by her friends.

The baby is presented and taken to the bath where it is rubbed with duck egg.

At the age of seven boys begin lessons at a school attached to a mosque. The first day is one to celebrate and you may see a boy on a horse being led to school, escorted by chanting children. In the early years schooling consists of learning the alphabet and verses from the Koran but, gradually, Arabic and Persian grammar, arithmetic, and some poetry are added to the curriculum. There is a strong discrepancy between the sexes. Boys are taught reading and writing, and an elementary under-standing of religion, arithmetic, history and geography. Later they make a more advanced study of the humanities and the sciences. Thus they have before them the prospect of numerous careers. Girls, in contrast, tend to have a purely practical education. It is normally restricted to the fields of medicine, and useful skills such as embroidery, song and dance. Few learn to read and write.

A boy's circumcision is the most important moment in his young life. It normally takes place when he is about the age of seven or eight. Neighbours will wish a boy the best of luck when they see him wearing a blue satin hat and a sash across his shirt; they know the operation is imminent. When the day arrives, he is paraded on a horse or a camel through the streets. The boy is then placed on a table while the barber prepares to do his work. While clowns and acrobats try to distract the child, he is held down while the barber swiftly

An ornate procession celebrating a Muslim wedding passes through the Hippodrome.

makes the cut with a sharp razor. From this moment the boy must obey his father and he is excluded from the harem. You can find out more about royal circumcisions in Chapter 9.

A marriage is another major cause for celebration. It is invariably arranged by the prospective mothers; the bride and her husband are given the most superficial consultation. The extent of the festivities accompanying the wedding depends very much on the wealth of the two families. Normally, there is a party at the baths, while, simultaneously, the groom's friends enjoy the excitement of dancing with gypsy girls who perform unveiled.

On the wedding day itself, often a Friday, the bride's father gives his daughter, dressed in all her finery, a girdle to symbolize her new status. She is then veiled and taken out of the house, mounted on a donkey and led through the streets by her friends and relations to her husband's house. In the evening, once the imam has pronounced the couple married, they are free to join the guests for a wedding feast, which usually consists of an enormous plate of rice tinted yellow with saffron. Eventually, the bride retires to the bridal chamber, closely followed by the groom, who is now given permission to remove her veil.

When the sultan's daughter marries, no expense is spared. The groom's presents are paraded through the streets to gasps of admiration from the crowds as they watch the bejewelled clothes, piles of gold coins, cases of jewels, not to mention hundreds of trays of sweetmeats, passing by. The privileged few are permitted to see the trousseau in all its splendour within Topkapi Sarayi.

THE DELIGHTS
OF TURKISH FOOD

The servants then served me with iced sherbert, a liquor much used by the Turks and commonly made with liquorice, orange juice, and water, of which when I had tasted, one of them flung out of a silver bottle with a long narrow neck water upon my hands and habit.

LORD CHARLEMONT, *TRAVELS IN GREECE AND TURKEY*, 1749

Turkish food is very good and you are strongly advised to try all the favourite dishes. Locals eat twice a day, at midday and at sunset. They like to consume a number of small dishes at their meals, served in rapid succession, normally seated cross-legged at a low table. The number of courses is an advantage if you are a guest, since there is so much choice. Rather disconcertingly, you will find that the Turks are quite unabashed at eating with their fingers, since the fork is unknown and they only use a knife and spoon as cutlery.

Turks take their meals seated on the floor and using their fingers instead of cutlery.

Turks eat prodigious quantities of meat. It is cooked in all sorts of ways: roasted or boiled, often cooked in butter or oil, but never in dripping or lard, since pork is strictly forbidden. The two most popular dishes are the kebab, often served with cabbage, marrow, spinach and onion, and pilau rice, which is cooked in meat juice. Chicken meat pureed in milk is also very popular.

Locals also love their vegetables, served cold in oil or hot in butter. Aubergine and courgettes, stuffed with meat and rice and wrapped in vine leaves, known as *dolma*, are a particular favourite. Layers of light pastry called *borek* are filled with cheese and then fried – these make delicious snacks.

The best bread is made from flour grown in Bursa or Bithynia, made

tastier by being dusted with opium, cumin and other spices. Alternatively, the dough can be made with butter and coated with beaten egg. Considering that the sea plays such a central role in Istanbul life, fish is eaten more rarely than you might expect, although you will find no shortage of mackerel, sea bass, oysters and crabs on offer.

Desserts of all kinds are very popular, the sweeter the better, and they tend to be eaten at all times of the day. You will often be offered compotes of stewed fruits, flavoured with musk and ambergris. Other favourites are semolina tarts made with honey and garnished with coconut and pistachios, cream of almond puddings, and light pastry covered in honey and raisins. There is a rumour that there is a new sweet and those lucky enough to have tasted it swear that it is totally delicious. It comes in the shape of a cube made from chopped dates, pistachios and hazelnuts, bound with gel, flavoured with rose water, mastic or lemon, and dusted with icing sugar. Some wit has named it Turkish Delight.

These appetizing dishes are accompanied by sherbet, a favourite refreshment of the Turks, drunk cold with the addition of ice that has been transported by mules from Mount Olympus. There are all sorts of flavours, including rhubarb, rose leaves, lemons, tamarind and grapes. Other popular drinks are syrup, grape juice, and *hosaf*, made from raisins, mead and rose water.

The lower classes have little knowledge of all these exotic dishes and drinks. They make do with a staple diet of bread, flavoured with onion and garlic, cheese and vegetables, with fresh fruit in summer, rice and soup in winter, and with little more than water to drink. Sometimes they might be able to stretch to offal and tripe. Having said that, one of the few places where the lower classes can feel the equal of their social superiors are the baths, which are extremely popular.

TURKISH BATHS

The Turks are devoted to washing their hands, their feet, their necks and all the body, including parts that I am too ashamed to mention.

THEODORE SPANDOUNES, *ON THE ORIGIN OF THE OTTOMAN EMPERORS*, 1523

Since you probably come from a country where washing more than once a week is considered downright dangerous for your health, you may already have noticed how much attention the Turks pay to personal hygiene. They are addicted to the baths, which they treat not only as a place to wash, but also as a social centre, a place to meet friends and exchange gossip. There are as many as 300 public baths in Istanbul, and possibly over 4,000 private ones. All major mosques have an attached bath, some of which are open to non-Muslims, and all have a strict segregation between men and women.

I *Sultan Mahmud, here dressed in all his finery, has been on the throne for 20 years.*

II (Following pages) *A distant prospect of Istanbul with Uskudar in the foreground.*

III *The magnificent dome of Ayasofya rises above a cluster of houses, with Turks promenading in the foreground.*

IV (Above) *Tapestry merchants go about their business on the banks of the Golden Horn.*

V (Following pages) *The Grand Vizier in a procession crossing the Hippodrome, depicted by Vanmour, with the Blue Mosque on the left.*

VI–VIII *Iznik pottery.*
(Above left) *This
bottle dates from the
best period of Iznik
pottery in the late 16th
century.* (Above right)
*A very fine, ornately
decorated Iznik vase in
the characteristic blue,
green and red colours.*
(Right) *This dish is
decorated with flowers,
a favourite Ottoman
theme for much of the
most beautiful Iznik
pottery.*

By origin the Turkish love of bathing harks back to the practices of the ancient Greeks and Romans. The *hamam,* as the Turks call a public bath, originally served as an annexe to a mosque, since a central tenet of Islam is that the worshipper should have washed and purified himself or herself before entering the house of Allah.

The grander baths are beautiful buildings, with a spacious domed hall inside the entrance that has a fountain in the centre and a raised platform around the walls where bathers leave their clothes. This is a room to relax in after taking a bath. The first room

> *Many fine women naked, in different postures, some in conversation, some working, others drinking coffee or sherbet, and many negligently lying on their cushions, while their slaves (generally pretty girls of seventeen, or eighteen) were employed in braiding their hair in several pretty fancies.*
>
> LADY WORTLEY MONTAGU

you enter from the hall is the *tepidarium,* heated by a continuous flow of hot, dry air that allows you to perspire freely. You can then pass through to an even hotter steamroom or *calidarium,* where you lie on a marble platform, known as the belly stone, heated from below by a wood fire. Visitors' experience tends to vary: some marvel at the way that your mind wanders in the shimmering, diffused light, while others complain bitterly at the way the attendant

The wonderfully atmospheric interior of the Cagaloglu Baths.

Turkish women spend a lot of time at the baths; this one, with her hennaed fingers and toes, is hard at work washing herself.

pummels your tired limbs. Finally, you can retire to a cooling room where you can splash yourself with cold water.

Women are particularly fond of baths, since it is one of their best opportunities to socialize outside their homes, to meet and exchange gossip. As Lady Wortley Montagu noted, the bath is 'the women's coffee house, where all the news of the town is told, scandal invented'. They often spend the best part of a day at the baths, washing, taking a meal, nibbling on stuffed vine leaves, cakes and desserts while drinking coffee and sherbet, enjoying a good gossip before a final wash. Turkish women take great care over their physical appearance. After bathing, they proceed to beautify themselves, washing their hair with egg yolk, dyeing their hair and nails with henna, applying make-up (consisting of a paste made from almonds and jasmine), and even putting on beauty spots.

If you are a female visitor to Istanbul and want to join in, this is your chance to indulge yourself. While your hair is plaited by a young woman, you can anoint yourself with all sorts of potions: depilatory creams of sugar syrup, and jars of honeyed unguents. Attendants will provide vials of attar of roses, and the balm of Mecca, guaranteed to soften your skin and leave your face free of wrinkles. It is, however, so

popular among the ladies of the harem – who, of course, have first pick – that there is always a shortage of supplies.

The bath is also likely to be where a mother chooses a bride for her son. If you see a veiled woman seated on the bath-keeper's divan, she will almost certainly be eying up a prospective daughter-in-law, a golden opportunity to inspect not only her physique but also her behaviour. Brides come to the baths to be washed before their wedding, attended by female friends and relatives from both families, who sing religious hymns and folk songs.

It is, of course, impossible not to be conscious of a sexual undercurrent with so much naked flesh on view, or covered with a token linen shift. If you fancy your own kind, the opportunities for sexual dalliance are, needless to say, limitless. But this applies also to heterosexuals. Many of the major baths have wine shops nearby where customers use every opportunity to ogle women entering or leaving the premises. Rumour has it that if a Turkish man wishes to sleep with his wife, she will go to the bath before midday, while he will attend in the afternoon.

MEDICINE

The small-pox so fatal and so general amongst us is here entirely harmless by the invention of ingrafting (which is the term they give it).... There is no example of any one that has died in it, and you may believe I am very well satisfied of the safety of the experiment since I intend to try it on my dear little son.

LADY WORTLEY MONTAGU
(ON RETURNING TO ENGLAND,
SHE PERSUADED THE BRITISH ROYAL
FAMILY TO INOCULATE THEMSELVES,
THOUGH THE PROCESS WAS TESTED ON
CONDEMNED PRISONERS FIRST)

As they take so much trouble over their hygiene, you might expect the Turks to know a great deal about medicine. In fact you should be extremely careful who you consult should you fall ill, since there are so many quacks practising, and many of their remedies smack of sheer superstition. For instance, if a

baby has convulsions, mother-of-pearl oil will be rubbed on its stomach; but, if this does not work, an exorcism will be recommended. Equally strange is the widespread custom of curing an illness by covering the head of the afflicted person, pouring hot lead into a pan of cold water and then holding it over his or her head. More sensible are remedies such as aniseed for digestion, infusion of bitter wood to restore the appetite, taking rhubarb as a laxative, and the smoking of herbs to relieve congestion of the chest.

There is also the complication of how a doctor treats his female patients. It remains something of a mystery. A French doctor who has a practice in

Despite her veil this Muslim woman is bartering hard to buy medicinal drugs in the Spice Bazaar.

[43]

town has recorded how he is only able to take the pulse of his female Muslim patients through a piece of thick muslin. Turkish women know much about medicine themselves, making use of inoculations against smallpox, showing an understanding of this deadly disease far superior to that of most Europeans. But this knowledge does not seem to matter where their husbands are concerned. Several doctors have recorded the extraordinary excuses that a Turkish woman will use if she has caught venereal disease from her husband in order not to blame him.

You may also find it more than a little disconcerting to discover that the barber who cuts your hair also acts as a surgeon and a dentist. It is not an attractive sight to enter his shop if you find him busy drawing customers' teeth and applying leeches to their bodies.

SEX AND SLAVERY

You may meet European men who have been living in Istanbul for a while who complain of their frustration in being unable to meet Turkish women. The more desperate may confess that they have consorted with prostitutes, of which there is no shortage. The majority are Greek, Jewish

With so many Muslim women unavailable and unapproachable, prostitutes do a good trade in the back streets of Istanbul.

and Armenian, and there are said to be several thousand brothels in the city. European sailors, who have few scruples when looking for sex, are said to engage cheap prostitutes in the barracks of the janissaries.

Frustrated Europeans can only dream of the possibilities on offer for Turkish men. Not only do they have the legal option of marrying four wives, but the richer ones also own slaves and it is common knowledge that many desirable slave girls end up in their master's bed. Although you'll be used to seeing slaves back home, you will have witnessed nothing like the distressing sight of the slave

Slaves, both black and white, are a common sight all over the city.

concubines from the harem. Not only are they highly trained, and naturally graceful, but they are also very well connected.

Some Turks, however, prefer slave boys. Circassians are reputed to make the best slaves (with a top selling price of 1,000 imperial crowns). They are prized for their beauty and modesty, and for their sharp wits and capacity for instruction. However, if you are looking for something more intimate, there is reputed to be nothing better than an Abyssinian boy. One writer describes how they are 'especially proficient at taking care of beds – that they adore fluffing up and arranging the mattresses and pillows'. Then, unable to contain himself, he rhapsodises: 'by which I mean bending over and sticking out the behind when serving (coffee), so as to make those present at the gathering hope for different joys and pleasures'. No wonder visitors are often warned of the danger of 'turning Turk'.

market near the Beyazit Mosque (you can find out more about the buying and selling of slaves in the following chapter). You may well succumb to temptation and go to ogle the beauties on display. But beware, since one frustrated onlooker recorded that he was left with 'no other option than to go to bed every night alone and grasping his knees until morning'.

However, the life of a slave girl sometimes brings benefits. If she has a child by her master the offspring will probably be given his or her freedom. And for a man a concubine has many advantages over a wife; not only will she be nubile, but she is also likely to be more submissive and obedient than a free woman – and she will not bring with her any interfering relations. The most sought after, naturally, are

On a more prosaic note the role of slaves, in general, is less to do with sexual gratification and more concerned with household chores. They are, of course, required to do their mistress's shopping, since it would be unthinkable for her to be seen haggling in the markets. Some slaves manage to better themselves. Many are freed on their master's death.

IV · MARKETS, COFFEE HOUSES AND OPIUM DENS

The idol the Turks worship is gold; and in all common affairs their ears are opened by that powerful deity.

SIR JAMES PORTER, *OBSERVATIONS ON THE RELIGIOUS LAW, GOVERNMENT AND MANNERS OF THE TURKS*

MARKETS AND BAZAARS

Istanbul's markets are one of the highlights of the city, where all your senses will be assailed at once, a vivid blend of colour, noise and smell. Be careful not to get lost when you first visit one, since they are teeming with activity, so crowded, as one traveller noted, that 'even if Jesus were to return and descend from heaven and wished to come to the city, he would not find space to leave even a needle'. Take advice from locals who will tell you where to find the best merchandise. Different races adopt different selling techniques: the Greeks are vociferous, calling out and gesturing furiously as you pass by; the Armenians and Jews are more subtle, approaching you with a smile on their face and a word of praise for their prospective victim; the Turks are more retiring, only coming to life when you show interest in their wares, so that you are all the more surprised when they produce from their pocket a jewel of unsurpassed beauty.

The most famous market is the Grand Bazaar, reputed to consist of over 4,000 shops and 2,000 ateliers. It was established by Mehmet the Conqueror shortly after hi conquest of the city in 1453. This vast stone building, so unassuming from the exterior, only reveals its character when you enter its portals. Initially, you can make little out in the subdued light filtered through the holes in the innumerable cupolas, but gradually your eyes adjust to the gloom. An Aladdin's Cave lies before you, a miniature town with a mosque, fountains, little squares and, above all, thousands of shops.

Your initial impression will be one of chaos, with hundreds of tradesmen accosting the seething mass of humanity that makes its way up and down the crowded streets. Porters push their way through, often accompanied by a horse or camel laden with their wares. But after a while you will begin to understand how this world works.

The bedesten, or jewellers' quarter, shows so much riches, such a vast quantity of diamonds, and all kinds of precious stones, that they dazzle the sight.

LADY WORTLEY MONTAGU

[46]

Every trade has its own particular place in the bazaar.

There is everything that you could desire: flowered brocades and velvets from Bursa, brightly coloured carpets from Anatolia, shawls and cashmeres from India. Exquisite tiles from Iznik compete for your attention with metalwork from Bosnia and Mosul, and beautiful illuminated manuscripts. Precious goods have been shipped over from Western Europe: mirrors from Murano, clocks studded with precious stones, elegant hats, and French perfume, much sought-after by ladies. From the east come beautiful silks and carpets from Persia, furs and amber from the north, and even the

A busy market scene with merchants congregated round a splendid fountain.

occasional bird of prey from Muscovy. The most exotic goods come from China: spices and drugs, and rare porcelain. Africa provides the lure of gold.

If you can find your way into the heart of this labyrinth, you will come to the central domed hall, called the Old Bedesten, which houses the most valuable wares: gold, brass and copper, antique jewelry and coins, glassware, ancient weapons, Byzantine pottery and figurines. This is a fascinating place to visit. Whatever the temperature outside, it remains cool in summer, warm in winter. With so much of value, the Bedesten is securely locked at night to deter thieves. Over the main gate is written, with delicious irony: 'Gain and trade are like a wild bird, which if it is to be domesticated by courtesy and politeness may be done so in the

The Spice (or Egyptian) Bazaar in Uskudar, filled with exotic spices from all over the Ottoman Empire, is a wonderful sight.

one of the finest buildings in the city, and you can already make out the original design of its courtyard in the shape of a horseshoe.

The slave market is at the south end of the Grand Bazaar near the Beyazit Mosque. The most prized nationalities are those on the northern borders of the Ottoman Empire: Circassians, Russians and Poles, though these are normally secluded from view, and you are more likely to see negresses from deepest Africa. The dealers, of whom there are reputed to be as many as 2,000, reside in the Buyuk Valide Han, and are a ruthless bunch. They encourage prospective buyers to examine every aspect of the men and women on sale, and you will see them inspecting their mouths for loss of teeth, before moving on to their legs, thighs and 'most secret parts'. Loss of

Bedesten.' The bazaar is open from 8.30 in the morning until 6 at night. If you tarry too late, carried away by the excitement of haggling for a good price, you will hear the unmistakable sound of the gatekeeper hammering his keys on the iron doors of the Bedestan, telling everyone within that it is time to lock up for the night. However tired you are, on leaving make sure you don't miss the mosque being built beyond the eastern entrance; it promises to be

It is difficult for many travellers to resist the temptation to go and have a look at the slave market.

THE SPICE BAZAAR

Also named the Egyptian Bazaar, since the majority of the spices come from Egypt, brought over on the annual fleet from Alexandria.

Housed in a T-shaped building sited next to the Yeni Valide Mosque.

Every booth is filled with an intoxicating aroma of spices, a rich mixture of coffee, incense, saffron and pepper.

You can buy pastes, powders and ointments in all shapes and sizes.

The stallholders will do their best to persuade you that the aromatic gum on display has been picked by the beautiful girls of Chios from mastic trees, that their henna will transform your fingernails, and their soap will do wonders to your skin.

They will also tell you that their aloes will perfume your coffee cups, their pastilles perfume your kisses, and their powders give your lover a true refinement of pleasure.

Moldavia, and cheese from Piacenza and Lombardy in Italy. The finest, light, odourless oil, highly prized by the women of the harem, is shipped from Crete. Further afield ships from Egypt bring much-valued salt, and vegetables, spices and sugar crystals from Alexandria. Compotes and sorbets are part of the tribute paid by the sultan's vassals in Walachia, Transylvania and Moldovia. Biscuits and sugared almonds are shipped from Venice. The fruit markets are particularly tempting, the vendors' stalls filled with lemons, oranges and limes from Chios, dates from Asia, and cherries from the Black Sea. Peaches and apricots come from Sinop in northern Anatolia, and pears and figs from orchards overlooking the Bosphorus.

All along the waterfront there are fish markets, the merchants, almost invariably Greek, selling a bewildering array of fish. You might recognize turbot, brill, pilchard, sole, plaice and salmon. There are also swordfish and tunny, which the Jews are adept at salting, lufer, only caught by night, mackerel from the Black Sea, mullet from the Bosphorus, and oysters from the island of Marmara. The salesmen behind their stalls cry out their wares, seemingly oblivious to the stench from the discarded fish guts scattered all around. This is where you are likely to hear typical Turkish oaths: 'By the roof of heaven', 'May the graves' black angel fry your soul', and 'By the sultan's soul and the hairy scalp of my mother'.

virginity lessens the price of a nubile girl. Before the buyer pays for a female slave, he is allowed to take her home for the night, in theory to see if she snores but doubtless to weigh up her other 'qualities'.

Everywhere you go in the city you will come across food markets. The produce on offer comes from all over the empire: meat from Anatolia and the Balkans, butter and salt from the Crimea, honey from Wallachia and

You can see, from the wily look on this merchant's face, why the Armenians are regarded as such good businessmen.

Every now and again you may see the stallholders looking a little nervous. The chances are that they have spotted one of the superintendents who patrol the market, ensuring that all is in order. Every Wednesday they are joined by the grand vizier, one of whose many job titles is market inspector. It is the superintendents' job to inspect the wares and attempt the well-nigh impossible task of preventing the stallholders from taking no more than a 10 per cent profit. If they apprehend a miscreant, he is immediately thrown on his back and the bastinado administered to his feet.

For several days afterwards he will be hobbling in considerable pain.

TRADE

Many of the city's merchants are either Greeks or Jews. The latter were formerly perfumers, blacksmiths and carpenters, but are now more often doctors, tax farmers, and officials in the city's customs office. Until recently, they dominated the banking trade, but bankers now tend to be Armenian, deemed to be more trustworthy. You may notice one of these newly rich figures, perhaps a member of the Serpos family, recent bankers to the grand viziers, in his quilted turban and fur coat, riding through the streets. The rich prefer to ride to work whereas in poorer areas you will see humbler artisans stepping over piles of rubbish in back streets as they make their way to their shops.

Much of the city's trade takes place down on the waterfront or in the area around the Beyazit Mosque where the Grand Bazaar is situated. On the quayside a common sight is an Ottoman official inspecting a ship's cargo. He will be accompanied by a janissary who will stay on board until the customs duty has been paid. As this amounts to between 3 and 5 per cent, the official will be keen to ensure that the captain is not hiding any of his goods.

There are dozens of *hans* in the city, most of them near the main markets. Combinations of inns and warehouses, it is well worth seeing at least one of them, since they are impressive buildings. The entrance is a great arched gateway, often with enormous iron doors as a protection from fire and thieves. This leads on to a courtyard with a fountain, surrounded by stables, and storehouses for every kind of merchandise on the ground floor, with galleries above where travellers sleep. Since they bring their own bedding, rugs and kitchen utensils, there is minimal furniture. Many of these hans contain an array of ancillary buildings including a kitchen, an eating room, baths and a mosque.

Whole streets are devoted to particular trades. Near the Beyazit Mosque you will find a street filled with coppersmiths, and workers in brass, iron and tin hard at work. They make quite a sight, with their grimy faces, sweating torsos, and dexterous fingers, twisting and hammering the metals into shape. Nearby are the turban-makers, metal-engravers, arms dealers and secondhand booksellers, where there was once a book and paper market during Byzantine times. The booksellers are notoriously mean and a frequent term of abuse in the markets is to call someone 'worse than a secondhand bookseller'. As you are enjoying the raucous haggling between purchasers and stallholders, make sure you avoid the horse-drawn wagons and porters forcing their way through the milling crowds. In the back streets sherbet-sellers from Anatolia are to be found

busily trying to sell their drink to women in exchange for kisses.

A city with such a flourishing trade is bound to attract merchants from all over Europe. It is vitally important that an ambassador to the Sublime Porte should obtain a coveted trade agreement, known as a capitulation, which enables his subjects to trade in Istanbul. The most successful are the French, who dominate trade with the Ottoman Empire. French merchants bring cloth, paper, glass and leather to Istanbul; in exchange they take home raw wool, hides, silk and luxury goods, including highly prized processed goat's hair, a vital component in the creation of wigs, without which no self-respecting Frenchman can be seen in public.

An occasional event, but one not to be missed, is a procession of the various trades in the city. A major one took place in 1736 and lasted six hours. At the front was an ox-drawn cart with a sower scattering grain, followed by a young man carrying the Koran, and then every sort of trade represented on triumphal carts: bakers, water-carriers, millers, goldsmiths, fishermen, mariners and butchers. Bringing up the rear were furriers, with rare skins displayed on poles.

Many trades are associated with distinctive costumes. You will come across water-carriers and sherbet-sellers in most streets in summer, wearing leather jerkins and black top-boots; there is no mistaking the sound of the clink of the glasses and metal cups that they keep attached to their waists. Often they are accompanied by a horse bearing a great leather jack on its back. In hot weather they cover the top with leaves to keep the water cool. The more accomplished have pipes inserted from which they draw the water. Other trades are instantly recognizable by their attributes; outside the doors of the dyers' shops hang brightly coloured silks drying in the sun.

COFFEE AND WINE HOUSES AND OPIUM DENS

Buyers and sellers alike take time to relax after their negotiations. The best place to do this is in a coffee house. When coffee arrived in Istanbul in the 16th century, the whole city became addicted to the new drink overnight. Coffee houses sprang up in every district. They tend to be strategically sited near the shops or a mosque, in a small square or at a busy junction. Most coffee houses are single-storey wooden structures, simply furnished.

Only men may enter these institutions, which serve as a combination of home and market, a place to conduct business or relax, playing backgammon or chess, or simply gossiping. Ironically, in the home it is the prerogative of the women to serve coffee, and a bride's ability to make good coffee is seen as an important factor when a Turkish mother is considering the qualities of her son's future wife.

The common room inside the entrance of the coffee house has small wooden chairs or raised divans where customers chat and drink coffee. One corner houses a kitchen, with a small furnace where coffee is brewed. In the opposite corner is placed a highly decorated divan, where the elders of the neighbourhood and important merchants can sit and disseminate news or tell stories. Sometimes you will find a mullah seated here, dispensing wisdom. In fine weather there are very often patrons sitting outside on benches in the sun.

These cafes are also a favourite place for smokers. Tobacco has been immensely popular in Istanbul since

A Turkish woman sits on a sofa smoking, a popular pastime for both sexes.

A great deal of male social life takes place in coffee houses, which are very popular.

it was introduced at the beginning of the 17th century. Pipes are a particular favourite; you can judge a smoker's status from the length and decoration of his pipe, or the mouthpiece he inserts into a waterpipe, or *narghile,* as it is known. Various sultans have tried to ban the habit in the past, but without success. Not only do they regard smoking as a vice, but they are also well aware of the number of fires caused by a smoker falling asleep with a lighted pipe, or having put it out carelessly, often after imbibing too much alcohol.

Nobody knows for sure how many coffee houses there are in Istanbul, but it has been calculated that one in seven businesses is run from one. There are about 100 on the Bosphorus, with 20 in the area of Besiktas alone. They vary enormously. Some are very respectable, others are much more louche, and you will find, of an evening, that the clientele are being entertained by dancers, either boys or girls, whose provocative and suggestive movements leave little to the imagination.

The authorities have a distinctly ambivalent view of coffee houses. They recognize their popularity, which makes them a valuable source of income. On the other hand, they can be havens of vice, and gossip can often turn to a discussion of the government, invariably critical. Many of them are owned by politically unreliable janissaries, and a number

The jugs are broken, the goblet empty, wine is no more
You've made us prisoners of coffee, alas destiny alas.

SANI

[53]

Opium can have a disastrous effect on users, as these addicts show all too clearly.

people take it, and it is even reputed to be used by mothers as a tranquillizer for their babies. In contrast, hashish, considered to be a stronger drug, is banned, although you will see the occasional addict, his face shrivelled and yellow, with no light in his eyes.

Another temptation is alcohol, which was explicitly banned by Mohammed in the Koran. A great many Muslims seem to take little notice of this, though they do not own taverns, which are the preserve of Greeks, Armenians and Jews. The most popular drink is *boza*, made from fermented millet. This is particularly attractive to those who have a guilty conscience, since it comes in two types, alcoholic and non-alcoholic, enabling the imbiber to pretend that he is not transgressing Muslim law.

There are numerous wine houses all over the city, especially in Galata, which is the Christian quarter and this home to a particularly thirsty population, and where the government inspector of wine has his office. You will soon locate them from the sound of music, singing and raucous laughter. These wine houses are widely regarded as dens of vice frequented by prostitutes,

of recent revolts have started in their coffee houses. As a result the government has passed regulations to try to control them, but most owners simply turn a blind eye to such rules.

If your taste is for something stronger than coffee, you will not have to look far to gain satisfaction. There are a number of opium dens in the city, particularly in the area around the Suleymaniye. You will see addicts in the surrounding streets, pale, sad-faced and puny. Although the use of opium is frowned upon, many

Near thy rubies, ne'er I bow my head to wine of rosy hue;

'Neath the shadow of the Magian priest, I ne'er the glass eschew.

Now it makes me the exile's prisoner, now the comrade close of pain –

What to do I know not, what with this sad fate of mine to do!

NEV-RES, 1760S

often male. As one regular put it: 'How could I know that prostitution was a lock and wine its key?'

Periodic attempts by various sultans to ban alcohol have had no more effect than similar bans on the use of tobacco. You will never hear it mentioned by a Muslim, but, despite their role as caliph and successor to Mohammed, a number of sultans have been addicted to drink. Beyazit II, known as the Thunderbolt, loved Shiraz wine. Selim I, nicknamed the Sot, had drinking bouts lasting for days. Murat IV, who was brutal in his attempts to suppress drinking, at least among his Muslim subjects, was often drunk himself.

GUILDS

Members of various trades and crafts are able to join a guild, which offers them mutual protection and support. Though the guild system is not as powerful as it once was, there are lodges and clubs in every quarter of the city, with their own rules and regulations. They meet every first and third Friday of the month, with officials with grand titles such as president, superintendent and inspector, presiding. Each guild also has an official of the imperial household assigned to it. The officials are responsible for the behaviour of its members, the maintenance of professional standards, the payment of dues and members' activities in the market.

A guild uses its own funds to provide loans to its members and to help sick colleagues. It distributes food to the poor, organizes prayer meetings and holds trade fairs. To join a guild, a youth must first serve an apprenticeship under a master, who will recommend him when he judges the boy ready to become a fully fledged member. Once a year each guild will hold a feast to which friends and family are invited. After the meal members are encouraged to sing and dance, and they and their guests will be entertained by acrobats and wrestlers.

Each guild has its own patron saint, a prophet or holy man taken from the Koran or the Old Testament, supposedly an expert in their particular calling. Abraham, the builder of the Kaaba in Mecca, is the patron saint of builders, Noah of shipbuilders, David of armourers and blacksmiths, Jonah of sailors and fishermen. Appropriately, Cain, who killed his brother Abel, is patron saint of murderers and gravediggers.

OTTOMAN COINAGE

The Turkish money is very good; they have gold, silver and mixed metal.
LORD BALTIMORE

You will have read of the complexities of Turkish money in Chapter 1, where the difference between the kurush, the para and the akche was described. But you need to be careful in your dealings with Turkish money. Ever since the Ottoman mint stopped producing silver akches, there has been considerably less control over the coinage, and indeed the whole Turkish economy. To give you an idea of what these coins are worth, an unskilled construction worker earns about 10 paras or 30 akches.

One of the main, and recurrent, problems is that the Turks like to use foreign coins, particularly Venetian and Dutch, as well as their own. This

They are naturally rather simple and dense, people whom one can easily deceive. So the Christians play an infinite number of dirty tricks and cheats on them.

JEAN CHARDIN, 17TH CENTURY

has led to much confusion, and has encouraged numerous counterfeiters. In fact mints in Livorno, Monte Carlo, Avignon and Orange have been set up to produce coins with an inferior metal content to flood the Turkish market. Unscrupulous merchants, of whom the Dutch are the most notorious, make enormous profits from using these coins, provided they are not caught. So take care that you do not end up with a bag of worthless coins at the end of your stay.

There have been a number of revolts due to arrears of pay or debased coinage. When the government runs out of money, desperate measures are taken to avoid the threat of chaos. Back in the 1620s Kosem Sultan, whose young son Murad IV had just ascended to the throne, melted down all available gold and silver in the palace to pay the troops she needed to ensure the peaceful succession of the new sultan.

The two sides of a kurush coin – this is standard silver coinage used throughout the Ottoman Empire.

PRICES AND TAX

As you gradually learn about the price of items in the shops, you will find that this is something the government is closely involved in. It controls the market by establishing fixed prices for food, commodities and luxurious items such as coffee, wine and even opium. This system of control includes checking the weight and

CONFUSION OVER RECENT COINS

In theory all coins contain the set ratio of 60 per cent silver to 40 per cent copper.

Silver coins minted in the 1690s were called 'new *zolotas*', to distinguish them from the Polish zolotas, widely used in Istanbul.

The Turks already had a coin called the kurush but, shortly afterwards, a new kurush was introduced, and weighing 6¼ *dirhams*.

The new zolota is valued at ¾ of the new kurush but they differ in weight and in the amount of silver they contain.

In Galata or Pera people usually refer to a kurush as a *piaster*, an Italian coin.

Gold coins recently introduced, close to the standard of the Venetian ducat, are called the *tughrali*, the *zincirli*, the *findik* and the *zeri mahbub*.

Now you can understand why you need to be careful in your financial dealings with the locals.

in overall control of prices, although in practice he delegates this to the market inspector.

There is much negotiation between government officials and members of the various trades, keen to make as much profit as possible, over these prices. They are announced by a public crier. One of the reasons why the government is so sensitive about prices is because it knows that economic unrest can lead to rebellion, and punishments can be severe for offenders. You may even witness the gruesome sight of a baker who has been grossly overcharging his customers strung up outside his bakery.

The authorities are well aware that the population is unhappy about the taxes it is made to pay. The situation is made more complex by the fact that there is no universal tax collection system. You may well find that if you ask half-a-dozen Turks, they all pay varying rates of tax. Different ethnic groups and religions pay different rates too. This divergence means that the system is wide open to corruption. For instance, Orthodox churches are permitted to raise taxes from their own communities. This means that a senior religious official will pay the Ottoman authorities a large sum of money to obtain a senior post, knowing that he can recoup the expense by charging tithes to his parishioners. It would be fair to say that the principle of tax farming has replaced tax collecting.

quality of goods, particularly bread, the most important of all basic foods. In addition, officials check that food is properly cooked, that pots are washed in clean water, and that animals are not overloaded. They also fix prices for trades such as porters and gravediggers. In theory the grand vizier is

V · SULTANS, GRAND VIZIERS, AMBASSADORS AND JANISSARIES

I who am the Sultan of Sultans, the Sovereign of Sovereigns, the distributor of crowns to the Monarchs of the globe, the Shadow of God upon Earth.

SULEYMAN THE MAGNIFICENT
BEGAN HIS LETTERS IN THIS MANNER

THE SULTAN

The sultan is supreme ruler of the Ottoman Empire, both in secular and religious matters, and all his subjects owe allegiance to him. All law emanates from the sultan, he is the caliph, or supreme religious ruler, and he is the commander-in-chief of the army. The present sultan, Mahmud I, is the heir to one of the most successful dynasties in history. From its beginnings in the 14th century, the Ottoman sultans (originally they called themselves beys) proved a series of able and aggressive rulers, carving out a kingdom that covered Anatolia and much of the Balkans. During the century that followed the conquest of Constantinople in 1453, no power could withstand the sultan at the head of his armies. Under Suleyman the Magnificent, who reigned from 1520 to 1566, the Ottoman Empire reached its greatest extent.

Gradually the sultan became more inaccessible, spending more and

more time enjoying the pleasures of life in Topkapi. To the outside world he is a remote figure. Although he is visible at audiences, at Friday prayers, and enjoying the pleasures of the Bosphorus in his caique, always dressed in fabulous costumes embroidered with cloth of gold and jewels, few people have ever heard him talk.

Mahmud I has reigned since 1730, when he was suddenly made sultan following the deposition of his uncle Ahmed III. He was 34 years old, and since his seventh birthday, he had been incarcerated in the Cage, the gloomy rooms in Topkapi assigned to unwanted sons and brothers of the sultan. He was, therefore, totally unprepared for high office. However, faced with a serious revolt by those who had deposed the sultan, and killed his grand vizier and grand admiral, he proved his mettle, and destroyed the rebels. The first few years of his reign were characterized by further revolts, which were put down mercilessly. The sultan has been accused of being 'mobile to every wind', and too reliant on his mother, Saliha, and his chief black eunuch Haci Besir Aga, which may account for the number of grand viziers he has disposed of.

> *The powerful are never so great as when they go to the help of the weak.*
>
> FAVOURITE SAYING OF MAHMUD I

RULES OF SUCCESSION

> *Of whichever of my sons God confers the Sultanate, it is proper that his brothers, for the sake of the order of the world, be slain.*
>
> MEHMET THE CONQUEROR

There was no law of primogeniture, therefore any son of a sultan could succeed.

Mehmet the Conqueror introduced the law of fratricide, where a new sultan immediately ordered the execution of all his brothers, by strangulation with a bowstring to avoid the shedding of royal blood.

From the reign of Selim I (died 1520) onwards the sultans ceased making dynastic marriages.

Instead, they took their pick from the slave concubines in the harem, all of them converted infidels.

The harem was a hotbed of intrigue as the women fought to ensure that their son succeeded to the sultanate.

When Ahmed I succeeded in 1603, the law of fratricide was commuted to one of incarceration – in the rooms in Topkapi known as the Cage.

> *Let me eat my chestnuts and strangle me afterwards.*
>
> ONE OF THE SONS OF MURAD III (WHO HAD 20 SONS, 19 OF WHOM WERE EXECUTED AFTER HIS DEATH – THE OTHER, MEHMED III, ORDERED THE EXECUTIONS UPON SUCCESSION)

Suleyman the Magnificent was the most successful of all Ottoman sultans; you can see the Suleymaniye in the background of this engraving.

Mahmud is now 50 years old. Although Lord Charlemont considered him to be 'of good countenance and of a graceful person', he is, in fact, a hunchback with rather short legs. Fortunately, this physical defect is much less apparent when he is mounted on horseback, which is how the public tends to see him. Mahmud possesses one further defect: he has failed to father any children

During the six years of his administration, one would have thought that he intended to exhaust all Europe of diamonds and purchase the whole produce of the mines of Golconda and Brazil.

SIR JAMES PORTER ON THE CHIEF
BLACK EUNUCH HACI BESIR AGA

despite the best efforts of his doctors, who have plied him with potions. After poring over their horoscopes, his astrologers have declared that he will never beget a child on land. As a result a number of concubines have been lined up for him on his yacht and a kiosk specially constructed in the Bosphorus. In addition a number of pleasure houses have been built for the sultan on the waterfront, with names such as the House of Joy and the House of Desire. However, none of these enticing experiments has so far proved successful.

Although the sultan lives in the seclusion of Topkapi, he knows that his subjects should have the chance to see him in the flesh. There are certain formal occasions such as his attendance every Friday at a mosque. The route he takes riding through the streets is well known, and this gives his subjects the chance to present petitions, which he receives very graciously from his horse. He also inspects his troops and the imperial fleet, though it is more likely you will see him when he takes to the waters of the Bosphorus in his caique.

The grand vizier is the second most important person in the empire.

THE GRAND VIZIER

The neck of a servant of the Sultan is thinner than a hair's breadth.

OTTOMAN SAYING

Since the sultan is so detached from everyday life, isolated in Topkapi Sarayi, it is his prime minister or grand vizier, the holder of the royal seal, who effectively runs the government. Over the years the post has been traditionally filled by a Christian, selected from the Palace School. His power base is called the Sublime Porte, just outside the Topkapi, where he lives in considerable style. As a measure of its importance, the formal title of a foreign ambassador is to the Sublime Porte, just as one in Britain is to the Court of St James's. The grand vizier's powers include all appointments to the army and the administration, he is responsible for law and order in the city, and he commands the army in times of war if the sultan chooses not to do so himself.

If you want to get something done, the Sublime Porte is where to head for. Just watch the swarms of petitioners, hoping to buttonhole the officials entering and leaving the building, and you will know you are at the right place. The throng is particularly thick when the grand vizier holds a divan, or audience, which he does three times a week. If you can fight your way through the crowd, you may be fortunate enough to see one of these in session. It is a court of appeal, with the grand vizier as supreme judge.

If you wish to visit the Sublime Porte, you can emulate Lord Charlemont, a recent visitor, who was advised by his dragoman Pisani 'to escape observation and consequent trouble, to disguise myself in Greek dress'. Thus attired, Charlemont was able to inspect the apartments of the Porte in great detail, admiring 'large, lofty and well-proportioned rooms' furnished with the 'finest silk Persian carpeting'. He watched the grand vizier seated on his throne, while an officer stood behind, 'holding in his hand a large plume or plume of feathers which he was incessantly waving about the Vizir's head to chase away the flies'.

Despite the appearance of splendour (the grand vizier is the only person, apart from the sultan himself, who is allowed to smile and bow to the left and right as he rides through the streets), the post is one of great insecurity, subject to the whim of the sultan, and the focus of any criticism of the regime. The present incumbent, Divitdar Mehmed Pasha, only succeeded at the beginning of the year, the 15th person to hold the position since Mahmud I came to the throne. From the Parade Pavilion standing opposite the Sublime Porte, the sultan can keep a close eye on who is visiting his grand vizier. A century

ago the mad Sultan Ibrahim used to sit at the window of the pavilion taking pot shots at passers-by with his crossbow. That was a particularly dangerous time for those with the temerity to hold the post of grand vizier: during a 12-year period between 1644 and 1656, there were 17 grand viziers, 15 of whom died violent deaths.

In 1730, during the Patrona Halil revolt, the grand vizier was decapitated and his body thrown out of Topkapi into the street. The janissaries, by then completely out of control, proceeded to dig up the body of the grand admiral Mustafa Pasha, whom they had killed, dragging his body through the streets to Topkapi tied to the tail of a donkey, leaving it to be torn apart by wild dogs.

One of the key posts is that of chief interpreter, known as the dragoman to the Porte. He is in a very powerful position since so few Turks speak foreign languages, and foreigners show a marked inability to learn any Turkish. This dragoman is traditionally a Phanariot Greek, and plays a key role in the conduct of day-to-day business between foreign embassies and the government at the Sublime Porte. He also translates foreign documents and extracts information from foreign news-sheets. The dragoman to the Porte is answerable to the grand vizier. However, his position

> *Though I am the sultan's slave, whatsoever I do is done. I can at a stroke make a pasha out of a stable-boy.*
>
> IBRAHIM PASHA, GRAND VIZIER TO SULEYMAN THE MAGNIFICENT

RANKS IN THE OTTOMAN HIERARCHY

The Ottoman system of government is strictly hierarchical – beneath the sultan and his grand vizier the key ranks are:

Aga, or head of an organization – the most important are the aga of the janissary corps and the chief black eunuch, powerful in Topkapi Sarayi.

Pasha is an honorary title bestowed on a high-ranking army officer or a senior civil servant – the captain pasha, in charge of the navy, is very powerful.

The chief dragoman to the Porte is a position of great importance.

Bey originally denoted a governor of a province – now it is simply means 'mister'.

Effendi is a similar rank, used for the grand vizier's personal assistants.

The head gardener (*bostancibasi*) is immensely influential – he supervises most activities in Topkapi, providing the sultan's bodyguard, grooms, porters and boatmen, carrying out disciplinary measures in the palace, and supervising food entering the kitchens.

Ranks in the Ottoman hierarchy were originally based on military status, indicated by the number of horse-tails attached to your standard: the sultan was given four, his grand vizier and chief black eunuch three, pashas or *beylerbeyis* (senior provincial administrators) two and beys just one.

Non-military ranks include the Sheikh ul Islam, who is head of the influential *ulema* (a religious institution), and the *kadi*, or judge in charge of interpreting Islamic law.

is very vulnerable, and the grand vizier, whose own position is equally precarious, will immediately blame him when there are problems with foreign powers. He is therefore widely known as 'the principal slave of the Porte'.

THE QUEEN MOTHER

Known as the valide sultan, the queen mother plays a very powerful role in Ottoman society. In the late 16th and early 17th centuries, she was, indeed, the most important person in the whole Ottoman Empire. Two exceptional women filled the role. The first

was called Nurbanu Sultan (1525–83), or Lady of Light, the favourite consort of Selim II, and mother of Murad III. She was a Venetian noblewoman called Cecilia Baffo, niece of the Doge Sebastian Venier, and captured by the Turkish admiral Barbarossa on the island of Paros. When her drunken husband Selim died in 1574, Nurbanu kept his body hidden in an ice-box until her son arrived in the capital, at the same time arranging for Selim's other five sons to be strangled. For the next nine years, she ruled the Ottoman Empire as valide sultan together with the grand vizier.

Even more powerful was Kosem Sultan (c. 1589–1651), daughter of a Greek priest and the favourite concubine of Ahmed I. After Ahmed's death, she ruled the empire as official regent from 1623 to 1651, arranging treaties, and receiving taxes and income from the provinces. She even accompanied her two sons Murad IV and Ibrahim the Mad to Friday prayers. When Ibrahim was deposed, she continued to rule through her grandson Mehmed IV. Like Nurbanu, she attended meetings of the divan from behind a curtain. When Kosem finally fell from power, she was strangled with a curtain by the chief black eunuch of the harem, Tall Suleyman. Because she had dispensed much of her great wealth among the population by fostering good works she was very popular and, after her death, the populace of Istanbul observed three days of mourning.

Since that time the valide sultan has never exerted the same amount of power, although she remains a formidable presence, hidden away in the seraglio, where she lives, like a spider in her web, controlling all around her. Her power, however, is ephemeral, and vanishes in a split second on the death of her son the sultan.

AMBASSADORS

As you would expect, the role of foreign embassies to the Ottoman government is one of great importance, with the prospect of benefiting from the lucrative trade that passes through Istanbul. There is a great deal of intrigue as the leading ambassadors jockey for position and favour. Ever since the 16th century, the French have held pride of place among the western powers, and, as we have noted in Chapter 4, they continue to dominate trade with Turkey (a generation ago the first embassy ever sent by the Turks themselves was to France). Obtaining permission from the government to trade in the empire, the key aim of all foreign nations, is given the esoteric title of Renewing Capitulations. Ambassadors see themselves as representing their sovereign and are constantly doing everything they can to demonstrate their nation's power. This involves putting on an impressive display from the moment of their arrival in the city, with a full retinue accompanied by military bands. You may well see an ambassador on an evening visit to one of his fellow diplomats, attended by running footmen holding torches.

One of the chief complications facing an ambassador is the difficulty of mastering the Turkish language and therefore his dragoman plays a key role. Although he is usually a Christian, the dragoman is a Turkish subject, and therefore liable to mistranslate conversations. He is also very often open to bribery and most ambassadors are only too willing to give inducements to make sure that their dragoman gives an accurate record when they have discussions with Turkish officials. Indeed, most ambassadors bring with them all sorts of gifts: gold and silver brocaded robes, boxes of perfume, mirrors, and guns, all of which are dispensed judiciously to secure favours. The French have attempted to bypass this system by sending a number of Christian youths to Paris so that they can be taught French, later to return to Istanbul to serve as dragomen.

These ambassadors live in great style in Pera. Their embassies are designed in the Turkish style, with a large upper reception hall, and rooms divided into men's and women's quarters. The rooms are furnished in the European taste, with, chairs, tables, presses and beds, and hangings of linen, silk and damask. Each embassy has its own chapel. On the ground floor are the stables, storerooms and bakeries. The French, ever anxious to impress visitors, have a throne room in their embassy, with portraits of the kings of France. Interestingly, despite this grandeur, and the close ties the French have with the Ottoman government, the Venetians, ancestral enemies of the Turks but always keen to promote trade with La Serenissima, have a bigger embassy, employing 118 staff, though 50 of these are priests.

The British ambassador is dwarfed by Ottoman officials during an audience with the grand vizier.

One of the key aims of all foreign ambassadors is to be granted an audience with the sultan, which takes place inside Topkapi Sarayi. If you have the opportunity, try to join your country's ambassador since this may well be your best chance of seeing inside Topkapi, though the audience may not be quite what you expect. One of the most extraordinary aspects is that the normal forms of diplomacy that characterize Western European ambassadorial meetings do not apply, and you may be shocked at the way that your representative is treated, ranging from indifference to rudeness. On occasion, ambassadors have even ended up in prison, the most recent being the Venetian and Austrian ones in 1714 and 1716 respectively.

To emphasize his power, the sultan often leaves an ambassador waiting for hours or even days even after they have entered Topkapi. Sir James Porter complained bitterly that the room where he was kept waiting was 'fit rather for the reception of a Polish Jew'. Before meeting the sultan, the ambassador is presented to the grand vizier, resplendent in a white satin robe and a turban bound with gold (his officials have robes of blue, yellow, green and violet, depending on their rank), with whom he dines, up to 50 dishes being served in quick succession. Finally, the summons comes.

Before entering the Throne Room the ambassador is compelled to don a heavy fur robe embroidered with gold and silver. He is then led forward by two servants, supporting his arms, just to make sure he is not foolish enough to attempt an assassination. The ambassador will then kiss the richly embroidered caftan, made of cloth of gold, that the sultan wears on these ceremonial occasions. The Grand Turk, as Europeans call him, is seated on a magnificent throne, facing sideways, so that a mere infidel cannot see his face. The sultan appears to take no notice, his gaze remote and inscrutable, as the ambassador presents his credentials. No word passes his lips but just occasionally he will give a nod of approval which is regarded as a great honour.

Ambassadors, who tend to be pompous and self-important, seethe with indignation at this behaviour but they know how important it is to secure a lucrative trading agreement. One way to impress his Imperial Majesty is to present him with lavish gifts. To give an example, those presented recently by the Dutch ambassador Cornelis Calkoen included satin and velvet coats, a box of expensive scented oils, two silver filigree flowerpots, a large crystal cabinet, a decorated case containing spectacles and pots filled with confectionary, a 10-foot telescope and last, by no means, least, two fire extinguishers. Calkoen's secretary Rigo reported back to his master that the sultan was so impressed with the crystal cabinet that 'his majesty opened and closed it at least thirty times to examine it'.

JANISSARIES

The Sultan trembles at a Janissary's frown.

LADY WORTLEY MONTAGU

Janissaries are a major presence in Istanbul. They were once the most feared fighting force in Europe, an elite, celibate corps trained as soldiers. The janissaries were originally drawn from a forced levy on children from Christian parts of empire (because the Koran did not permit the enslavement of Muslims), but by the 17th century Muslims were being introduced into the corps. This consists of 196 regiments, numbering some 40,000 men, who are a ferocious-looking bunch, sporting long moustaches. It will not be long before you see them swaggering down the streets of Istanbul, wearing tall, white linen hats, dark-blue coats, and red, yellow or black boots according to their rank. Their barracks are situated between the Suleymaniye and the Golden Horn.

The janissaries also serve as a police force and control all security in the city. They themselves are governed by their own laws, and therefore answerable to no man. The government has a deeply ambivalent view of them. In public they cannot put a foot wrong, a recent proclamation referring to them as 'a great corps composed of brave champions of the faith, on which rests the blessing of him who is the Shadow of God on Earth'. In private, however, the government shares the view of the general population and the janissaries are castigated for their arrogance and refusal to submit to orders. As one irate commentator put it, they are no more than 'pastry-cooks, sailors,

The janissaries, in their colourful uniforms, are one of the sights of Istanbul. You will see them all over the city, but you should be cautious of making an approach.

fishermen, owners of coffee-houses and brothels'.

It is well known that janissaries are some of the best-fed of all soldiers. They care so much for their food that their officers bear ranks such as chief soup-maker, head cook, black scullion and head water-carrier, and it is the ultimate disgrace if the regimental cauldron is lost. On the numerous times when they have risen against their masters, the revolt invariably begins on pay day when the janissaries overturn their soup cauldrons in the First Court of Topkapi Sarayi.

However, despite their acute sense of self-importance (they are reputed to know of 60 ways to tie a turban), some janissaries have fallen on hard times and you may well find that your servant is one. The sultan himself now employs them as falconers, gardeners and oarsmen of the royal pinnace, and some are even given such menial tasks as dog handlers, woodcutters and navvies. Consequently, the janissaries' rate of pay has declined, and they have increasingly turned to trade to bolster their income.

They own a large number of coffee shops that are an ideal base from which to monitor the city's markets, which is one of their privileges. It is from a janissary's coffee shop, for example, that the powerful 56th regiment supervises the distribution of food entering Istanbul, the market for

They make and unmake emperors as the Praetorian guard did at Rome.

LORD BALTIMORE

timber and other construction materials, and fuel for heating.

There are, of course, all sorts of opportunities for less salubrious activities. The janissaries are famous for performing extortion, often forcing residents of an area to pay protection money. The normal method is to hang an axe, with the symbol of a particular regiment on it, over the door of a house or shop. If the owner refuses to pay the requisite sum of money, the janissaries will threaten to burn down his house. If you enjoy the view from one of these coffee shops, perhaps set on the city walls, you will note how

The charismatic figure of Patrona Halil, leader of the rebellion against Ahmed III.

the owner keeps a careful eye on shipping entering the Bosphorus or the Golden Horn. Doubtless he is working out if he can exact some tribute from a new arrival. Not so long ago, when an admiral objected to paying extortion money to a janissary for mooring rights for his ship, he was humiliated to find that his ship had been towed to the waterfront where it was moored for all to see outside a janissary coffee shop.

If you are in any doubt about the power of the janissaries, just look at Istanbul's recent history. They have forced the resignation of both Mahmud's predecessors; indeed, the rebellion of Patrona Halil against Ahmed III started in a janissary coffee shop in 1730.

THE ARMY AND REBELLION

God Almighty says 'I have an army which I have named the Turks. Whenever I am angry with a people I unleash the Turks upon them.'

ARABIC SAYING

Until recently, the Ottoman Empire was the greatest military power in the world, but there has been a gradual withdrawal in the face of constant threats from aggressive neighbours: the Austrians to the west, seeking to regain their empire in the Balkans, lost to the Ottomans in the 16th century; the Russians to the north, desperate to establish a base on the Black Sea; and the Persians to the east, perennial

enemies of the Turks. For the past four years the empire has been at peace, and you are unlikely to see the grand sight of the sultan setting off on campaign at the head of his troops, accompanied by a throng of attendants.

Nevertheless, it is well worth seeing the army in training. It makes a splendid sight, a glittering spectacle involving thousands of janissaries, with their copper spoons stuck in their turbans, the senior officers wearing heron plumes, their horses covered in velvet and gold, with henna-dyed horsetails waving from their spears, and an immense array of weapons, ranging from scimitars, lances, and bows and arrows, to muskets and cannon, dragged along by straining cannoneers. But the sultan is all too aware that it is not numbers alone that will win him wars. He needs to introduce much-needed reform of the armed forces, and, in particular, to learn from the European powers, with their superior technology.

To this end, a few years back the sultan instructed the Comte de Bonneval to do the job for him. Although Bonneval, or Ahmed Pasha, as he became known, had some success, he had a number of underlying problems to overcome. He had to answer to the grand vizier but the sultan kept dismissing them, and each new incumbent had his own ideas. In addition, the janissary corps was averse to change and this severely handicapped the Frenchman's ability to reform the system.

AN EXTRAORDINARY SOLDIER

The sultan's most remarkable general was a French adventurer born in 1675 as Claude Alexandre, Comte de Bonneval. He started his military career by serving as an officer in the Royal Guard of Louis XIV.

Unfortunately he was possessed of great insolence and an ungovernable temper.

Court-martialled and sentenced to death, he fled to Germany and became a major-general in the Austrian army under Prince Eugene of Savoy, fighting bravely against the French.

Falling out with his Austrian employers, he was court-martialled a second time and sentenced to death, commuted to banishment by the Austrian emperor.

He offered his service to the Ottoman government and converted to Islam.

Ahmed Pasha, as he became known, was appointed commander of the Turkish artillery.

Nicknamed Humbaraci ('bombardier'), he helped the Ottomans fight successful campaigns against the Austrians and Russians.

Bonneval was also a friend of many of the great figures of the age, including Casanova and the philosophers Montesquieu and Liebnitz.

He died three years ago in Istanbul in 1747.

A man of great talent for war, eloquent with turn of elegance and grace, very proud, a lavish spender, extremely debauched and a great plunderer.

A CONTEMPORARY ACCOUNT OF THE COMTE DE BONNEVAL

One of the reasons why the sultan has been so keen to introduce reforms in the army is because he feels his position to be insecure. Recent wars have been very expensive and have led to much discontent. If you suddenly see shopkeepers shut up shop during normal trading hours you will know that trouble is brewing. You had best beat a hasty retreat to your quarters.

A shortage of food is another obvious cause for discontent. This is always more evident in wartime, when essential supplies are diverted to the army in the field. No wonder the government strives so hard to ensure the delivery of regular supplies. It knows full well the reaction if the wheat is 'black, full of soil and, stinking', as has happened more than once. One sultan was deeply humiliated when a group of Turkish women, incensed at the scarcity of food, marched through the streets carrying poles, topped with liver and guts, to the Beyazit Mosque, where they presented a petition to him.

LAW AND ORDER

There is not, I believe, in Europe any city where the police is so well regulated as at Constantinople.

LORD CHARLEMONT

Until you have lived here for a while, life in Istanbul appears very strange, and you may find the concept of Turkish justice difficult to understand. You may have heard of tales about the arbitrary behaviour of the sultans, their legendary cruelty, executing people on a whim, and indulging in torture. In Topkapi it is said that if the sultan opens the latticed window above the divan, or stamps his foot during an audience, it is a signal for immediate execution, normally by strangulation. And you may even see the decapitated head of an official displayed in a niche outside the Imperial Gate (more important ones are mounted in the First Court).

But this is not the complete story. The sultan is head of state, a remote figure hidden away for most of his life in Topkapi Sarayi. However, he likes to present an image that he is always open to his subjects, and he will receive petitions when he is in the divan, or on the streets riding to a mosque to attend Friday prayers. Some of the petitioners have travelled from the far reaches of the empire, and wish to tell their sovereign of their suffering from famine or poverty, or the seizure of their goods and enslavement of their women by enemies crossing the frontiers. More often these petitions deal with the extortionate behaviour of corrupt tax collectors, and even make accusations about the incompetence of government ministers including the grand vizier himself. Not surprisingly, the vizier makes strenuous efforts to intercept the petitions before the sultan can receive them.

The legal system is complicated because it derives from different sources. The sultan issues decrees, but more important is the Sharia, the sacred law of Islam based on the Koran, which affects every aspect of daily life, and is constantly updated by supplementary regulations. The influential body that administers religious law is called the *ulema*, a group

A mufti is an important figure, one of the most senior Muslim clergymen.

of learned men who run the mosques. They are easily distinguished by the white muslin wound round their skull caps. The ulema occupy a popular post since they are not subject to taxation. There are four ranks: Sheikh ul Islam, muftis, imams and mullahs. To give you some idea of the power of the Sharia, the sultan must gain permission from the Sheikh ul Islam before declaring war, imposing new taxes, and even banning the licence of printing presses (which is one of the reasons why you will find relatively few books in Istanbul). After Murad IV had made strenuous attempts to enforce a total ban on tobacco a century ago, it was the Sheikh ul Islam who lifted the ban, so all natives of Istanbul owe him a deep debt of gratitude for what constitutes one of their principal pleasures. You will find more information about Islam, the Sharia and the roles of different religious officials in Chapter 8.

They tell us of some rare examples in Turkey of uncorrupt judges; I have heard of one, but I have known none.

SIR JAMES PORTER

If you find the legal system rather confusing, you may also be shocked by the strain of cruelty that is a part of daily life. You will hear gruesome tales of dishonest merchants nailed by their ears to their shop fronts, or false witnesses forced to parade through the streets, sitting backwards on an ass holding the tail, while the entrails of a bullock are poured over them. You are unlikely to see thieves bound to the mouth of a cannon which is then fired into the sea, once a traditional punishment; instead the thieves are made to swallow a string with a stone attached to the end which is then pulled up violently, making the offender sick.

Executions, normally by beheading, usually take place in the early hours, so you are unlikely to come across the sight of the guilty man blindfold on his knees, being despatched by the executioner with one stroke of his sword. But you may see a corpse hanging outside the door of a house. The reason for this is that, after an execution, the executioner goes round the neighbourhood, knocking on doors, and asking for a token gift. When someone is brave enough to refuse, he will hang the body outside his door. After three days it is taken down and placed on a gibbet. Occasionally, a more gruesome death awaits the offender. He is stripped to his linen breeches, his hands bound behind his back; he is then drawn up by a rope on a pulley onto the gallows, and dropped onto an iron hook, and left there to die. In contrast the fate of guilty women is less gruesome, with drowning the usual method of execution.

And yet the system works. In each neighbourhood there are officials who know exactly what goes on in their locality. They punish offenders, control immoral activity such as prostitution, and in times of disturbance report anything suspicious to the authorities. These officials run patrols at night, led by a constable of the watch, which are very effective in deterring wrongdoers. These nightwatchmen move around the streets in silence and carry dark lanterns, which they only uncover when they apprehend a miscreant. They are particularly on the look-out for unknown men entering a woman's house. If one is spotted, he will soon be apprehended and taken away. If you are tempted to have an assignation with a Muslim woman, be very careful; the punishment for both parties is death. If the nightwatchmen catch a thief, he will be punished by the loss of a hand, or by the bastinado, being beaten with a stick on the soles of his feet, a very common punishment.

Lord Charlemont, who was here only last year and therefore an excellent judge of the current position, was impressed by the law-abiding behaviour of the Turks: 'There is not, I believe, in Europe any city where the police is so well regulated as at Constantinople. Housebreaking and street robbery, crimes so unfortunately common in our great towns as to render the dwelling in them unpleasant and unsafe, never happen in the Turkish metropolis, and a man may walk in streets at all hours of the night or even sleep in them with his pockets full of money, without the smallest fear or danger of molestation.' This is in stark contrast to the 'brutal acts of violence' that he considered were characteristic of towns in Western Europe.

However, despite his lordship's rose-tinted view, Istanbul is by no means free of crime. Violence and theft may be relatively rare, but bribery and corruption are much more common, with all ranks of society involved. As the Turkish proverb has it, 'The fish stinks first at the head'. There are frequent cases of witnesses being bought, and the signature on documents being forged. It is, of course, important to remember that if you have dealings with an official of the law, even a senior figure such as a judge, you should be prepared to offer him an inducement. You will find that an accused will often escape punishment in court if he hands over a sum to be divided between the prosecutor and the judge. One of the reasons that this is so prevalent is because judicial offices are sold to the highest bidder. Consequently, the successful applicant is very keen to recoup his money, the easiest way being to take bribes from those who appear before him.

VI · MUST-SEE SIGHTS

There is so much to see in Istanbul that you are spoilt for choice. Many of the best sights are in the Sultanahmet area near Topkapi Sarayi. To sample the full depth of Istanbul's history and culture, some of the finest mosques have been selected for inclusion in this guide, some large (Ayasofya, the Blue Mosque and Suleymaniye) others much smaller (Kucuk Ayasofya, Kariye and Rustem Pasha). Three of these (Ayasofya, Kucuk Ayasofya and Kariye) were formerly Byzantine churches and this is indicative of the richness and antiquity of the artistic culture of Istanbul. You will need to be very careful if you want to visit these mosques: non-Muslims are forbidden, so you will need to don a disguise and, preferably, go with a sympathetic Muslim who will show you what to do. And make sure that you do not go on a Friday or during a time of prayer. You will find more information about Islam and mosques in Chapter 8. Apart from religious buildings, sights have been chosen that show the incredible cultural variety of the city: the ancient Hippodrome, the imposing Land Walls, the beautiful Cagaloglu Baths and the Galata Tower, a landmark wherever you go.

At last the holy morn had come, and the great door of the newly built temple groaned on its opening hinges, inviting Emperor [Justinian] and people to enter; and when the interior was seen sorrow fled from the hearts of all, as the sun lit the glories of the temple.

PAUL THE SILENTIARY ON JUSTINIAN'S ENTRY TO AYASOFYA AT DAWN ON CHRISTMAS EVE 563

AYASOFYA (HAGIA SOPHIA)

Ayasofya is the greatest mosque in Istanbul – this is certainly what Muslims think, though Christians beg to differ. They cannot forget that it was, for almost 1,000 years, perhaps the greatest church in Christendom. The present mighty edifice was built by the emperor Justinian in just five years, from 532 to 537, a quite incredible feat of engineering.

For the Byzantines Hagia Sophia (as they knew it), with its vast, shallow dome, was an 'earthly heaven, throne of God's glory'. This was proved incontrovertibly by the building's near-miraculous ability to withstand earthquakes. Greeks still take pride in the fact that the orientation of the basilica, or mosque as they are meant to call it, is in the direction of sunrise at the time of the winter

JUSTINIAN

Under Justinian (527–65) the Byzantine Empire reached its greatest extent. His brilliant generals Belisarius and Narses reconquered much of the old Roman Empire, including Greece, the Balkans, Italy, Syria, Palestine, most of North Africa and southern Spain.

Justinian was a great law-giver – his codification of all existing Roman law was printed in the *Corpus Juris Civilis.*

The emperor was ably assisted by his formidable wife Theodora – she had been quite a girl in her youth, an ex-courtesan reputed to have known every trick in the book. Procopius in his *Secret History* quotes her as saying that her biggest regret was that God had only given her three orifices for pleasure.

Justinian presided over a golden age in the arts, his greatest work being the great building of Hagia Sophia – when it was completed the emperor declared 'Oh Solomon, I have surpassed thee'.

His subjects were less than enthusiastic about the vast amounts of money spent on Justinian's extravagant patronage of the arts, a major cause of the Nika riots.

emperor, joined the throng of fearful citizens in a silent vigil of prayer, with the Ottoman hordes gathered outside the walls. The next morning the emperor died fighting on the ramparts during the final Ottoman assault. When Mehmet the Conqueror rode into the city, ignoring the scenes of plunder and destruction being wrought by his victorious troops, he headed straight for Ayasofya to celebrate his triumph, and ordered the church's immediate conversion into a mosque.

Muslims and Christians alike will appreciate the beauty of the architecture, and no expense was spared on the decoration. You can admire columns made of red and green porphyry and verde antique marble, with delicate carvings of acanthus leaves and other foliage, and exquisite Byzantine mosaics in the nave and the galleries upstairs. Even the most disreputable emperors appear resplendent in the mosaics: Leo VI, who had four wives, his brother Alexander, who died of apoplexy after a short reign during a drunken game of polo, and the empress Zoe, whose enemies accused her, with some justification, of being a power-mad nymphomaniac. They and their fellow emperors once sat on a beautiful throne on the patterned marble coronation square, known as the centre of the world, next to the marble platform where the imam now reads from the Koran. You can see the greatest of the emperors, Constantine the Great and Justinian, as you leave Ayasofya by the

solstice, and not towards Mecca, as all mosques are meant to face.

One of the most poignant moments in the building's long history occurred on the night of 28 May 1453, when Constantine XI, the last Byzantine

The cavernous interior of Ayasofya (known to the Byzantines as Hagia Sophia) is even more splendid than the exterior; it is amazing to think that it is over 1,200 years old. It has been a mosque for a mere 300 years.

Vestibule of the Warriors, where the emperor's bodyguard waited while he worshipped inside. They are depicted in a mosaic above the door, presenting the city of Constantinople and the church of Hagia Sophia to the Virgin seated between them.

A building of this fame and antiquity attracts all sorts of legends. You will see a crowd of worshippers surrounding the column to St Gregory the Miracle Worker in the northwest corner. Women fervently believe that if they kiss the brass that sheathes the column, or rub a part of their body against it, it will increase their fertility, while men hope that it will cure their eye diseases. One of the most romantic legends recounts how a Byzantine bishop who was saying mass at the moment the Turks broke through the doors of the basilica in 1453. Climbing up the stairs to the gallery he disappeared through a small door that turned instantly into a stone wall. Try as they might, the Ottoman soldiers were unable to break through. It is said that on the day the basilica returns to Christian worship, the bishop will emerge from the door and continue the mass from the moment he left off.

Following Mehmet's lead, Ottoman architects have always paid due respect to this great building. It is said that Sinan, the greatest Ottoman architect, spent his whole career trying to surpass it (see the Suleymaniye, below). Sultan Murat IV was a particular admirer, and had a wooden enclosure filled with nightingales installed outside the south door, so that he could listen to

Glory to God, who has judged me worthy to complete this work. Solomon, I have outdone thee.

JUSTINIAN

their song while he attended Friday prayers. When the imam climbs the mihrab to read from the Koran, he holds in his hand an unsheathed scimitar to show that the mosque was acquired by conquest.

It is no wonder that the sultans have wanted to be buried here. Outside the building you can admire a number of their tombs, decorated with beautiful Iznik tiles, and four slender minarets. Just recently a charming fountain with a Chinese-style roof for performing ablutions was erected in the southeast corner of the complex.

BYZANTINE MOSAICS AND THE ICONOCLASTS

Making mosaics is an incredibly intricate business, involving the placing of thousands of individual tesserae (pieces of glass) in an elaborate pattern.

It is also very expensive, with lavish use of gold.

For centuries the Byzantine school of mosaicists was regarded as the best in the world, and their services were in demand all over the Mediterranean.

The mosaics in Ayasofya are truly wonderful, all dating from after 843 – ones before that date were destroyed by the Iconoclasts who ruled for the preceding century.

THE BLUE MOSQUE

*Oh, God, this is the service of your slave
Ahmed, let it be acceptable in your sight.*
AHMED I

Sultanahmet Camii, or the Blue
Mosque, as it is generally known, with
its cascade of domes and semi-domes,
is one of the great treasures of Istanbul.
If you are in the vicinity on a Friday at
noon, you may see Mahmud I coming
in a splendid procession to offer up his
prayers to God. An iron chain hangs
from the western entrance to the court;
the sultan is the only person who is

*The dome and minarets of the Blue Mosque
dominate the hill of Sultanahmet.*

allowed into the vast court on horseback and he is obliged to bow his head
to avoid the chain as he passes through
the gateway. A century ago he would
have been greeted by the sight of 30
officials strung up from the plane tree
that stands in the centre of the courtyard. The sultan then dismounts onto
a footstool of rich brocade, and, after
performing his ablutions, goes inside
the mosque.

The interior, covered in some 20,000
blue Iznik tiles, mostly of varying tulip
designs, provides a worthy setting for
such a mighty monarch to commune
with his God. If you look carefully at
the chandeliers, you will notice that
they contain some ostrich eggs. The
reason for this is the belief held by

Muslims that spiders are allergic to them and so cobwebs can be avoided.

Building a grandiose mosque is not always a good idea, particularly if you have failed to win any military victories that would have provided the funds to pay for it. Sultan Ahmed I was excessively proud of the building, erected between 1609 and 1616, and was even seen helping the workmen, his precious robe filled with earth. The locals were much less enthusiastic, complaining bitterly at the heavy taxes they were obliged to pay at the same time as their vainglorious sultan was reputed to be indulging himself in orgies with very fat, black girls. Much criticism was directed at the fact that this was the only mosque to have six minarets, which pious Muslims claimed was a sacrilegious attempt by Ahmed to rival the architecture of Mecca itself. The sultan, unabashed, ordered an extra one to be built at the mosque in Mecca.

From the moment it was finished, in the year of Ahmed's death, the closeness of the mosque to Topkapi Sarayi has meant that it has played a key role in Ottoman politics. The sultan's successor Mustafa I was an imbecile and was soon replaced by the young Osman II, but when he proved no better, it was in the Blue Mosque that leading politicians and figures at court met with the janissaries to plot his removal. Just 50 years ago a similar scene occurred leading to the deposition of Mustafa II. The mosque has also been the scene of revolt. In 1648, when the elite sipahis refused to set off to fight the Venetians in Crete, they were slaughtered here by the janissaries and such was the carnage that the marble of the walls turned red with their blood.

Don't miss the tombs just outside the mosque precinct. They include the extraordinary Kosem Sultan, wife of Ahmed I, her son the great warrior Murad IV and his unfortunate half-brother Osman II.

IZNIK CERAMICS

The town of Iznik, east of Istanbul, became the centre of a thriving ceramic industry in the late 15th century.

Inspired by Chinese porcelain, Iznik craftsmen produce bowls, jars and tiles of the highest quality.

They are made of a creamy mixture of clay and water, with a transparent glaze – not pure porcelain, whose secret remained the sole preserve of the Chinese for centuries (although the process has also been gained recently by the Saxons at Meissen).

The characteristic colours of Iznik ceramics are cobalt blue and white, sometimes with the addition of green and a vivid tomato red.

The decoration of the Blue Mosque consumed the production of the whole Iznik factory for many years.

Aside from the Blue Mosque, look for Iznik tiles of the highest quality in Topkapi Sarayi, the Suleymaniye and the Rustem Pasha Mosque.

THE HIPPODROME

The Hippodrome, the square in front of the Blue Mosque, has witnessed some of the most eventful episodes in Istanbul's history, though it is now a less salubrious area, particularly at night when handsome youths are reputed to come here to meet their lovers. From the moment Constantine inaugurated his capital on 11 May 330, this is where emperors and generals celebrated their triumphs, and where the Byzantines came to mock the remains of deposed rulers.

In earlier times the Hippodrome was famous for its chariot races, watched by up to 100,000 fanatical supporters. The Byzantines, like their Turkish successors, had a passion for horses, and the fanaticism of the supporters often led to trouble. The sculptured reliefs on the marble base of the ancient Egyptian obelisk in the centre of the square show this very clearly. They depict key events in the Hippodrome, including Theodosius the Great and his family watching a chariot race.

If you have visited Venice, you may have admired the splendid bronze horses over the facade of the Basilica of St Mark's. They held pride of place in the Hippodrome before the Venetians looted them during the Sack of Constantinople in 1204. Under the Ottomans the Hippodrome has been used for a variety of different types of ceremony. Back in the 16th century locals enjoyed a 52-day-long festival here to celebrate the circumcision of the sultan's son.

Greeks with a sense of history can admire the Serpentine Column at the southwest end of the Hippodrome,

rumoured to have once stood in the sacred Temple of Apollo at Delphi, as a thanksgiving for victory at the epic battle of Plataea in 479 BC, when the Greeks inflicted a decisive defeat on the invading Persians. Brought to the city in AD 324 by Constantine, not everyone has treated this column with due reverence; one night in April 1700 a drunken member of the Polish Embassy decapitated the serpents' heads.

On the west side of the Hippodrome stands the palace of Ibrahim Pasha, Suleyman the Magnificent's grand vizier at the apogee of the Ottoman Empire. Ibrahim used to invite his friend the sultan to watch guild parades and other festivities from the balcony of the palace. Such was his confidence that he placed statues of pagan gods Hercules, Apollo and Diana outside the palace, much to

The Hippodrome is the centre of many of Istanbul's festivities.

CHARIOT RACING AND THE NIKA RIOTS

Under Byzantium the Blue and Green factions were bitter enemies and fanatical supporters of their respective chariot teams.

The Blues represented the conservative upper and middle classes, while the Greens were champions of the radical lower classes.

The most severe riot between the two factions took place in 532 and reached a tragic conclusion when the Justinian's great general Belisarius slaughtered 30,000 members of the Green faction in the Hippodrome.

the amazement of pious Muslims. However, as in the case of so many grand viziers, his position was more precarious than it seemed, and his magnificent lifestyle aroused the jealousy of Suleyman's wife Roxelana. She was determined to remove her rival, and spent many hours whispering poisonous thoughts into the ear of her husband. One night in 1536, after he had enjoyed an intimate supper with his master, Ibrahim Pasha was strangled by mutes on Suleyman's orders.

On leaving the square, don't miss the extraordinary underground cistern off the north side. Known as the Basilica Cistern, or Yerebatan Sarayi, this astonishing construction (one third of the length and half the width of the Hippodrome) dates back to the time of Justinian, and was used to supply water to the Byzantine emperors' palace. It was discovered by accident by the French antiquarian Petrus Gyllius in 1544. He said of his visit, 'I boarded a small boat, in which the householder, holding lit torches, rowed me back and forth through the columns, as if through a forest, which stood quite deep in open water.' There are other vast cisterns under the city, supplying water for houses, shops, baths, fountains, and irrigating gardens and orchards – but the Basilica Cistern is the biggest.

This view of the Yerebatan Sarayi, formerly a Byzantine cistern, shows what an atmospheric place it is to visit.

THE KUCUK AYASOFYA MOSQUE

This is one of the most beautiful smaller mosques in Istanbul, formerly a Byzantine church called Saints Sergius and Bacchus dating back to the time of Justinian (Sergius and Bacchus were Roman soldiers martyred for their faith). One of a number of churches in the city converted into mosques, its plan is an unusual octagonal shape; the carving of the columns and capitals is very fine. The conversion was paid for by the powerful Huseyn Aga, chief black eunuch in the harem, in the early 16th century.

THE LAND WALLS

The construction of this massive line of fortifications represents one of the most extraordinary acts of desperation in history. Constantinople seemed to lie open to the hordes of Attila the Hun

after an earthquake had devastated the walls in the early 5th century. But, inspired by the emperor Theodosius II, the citizens worked night and day to rebuild them in just two months. For the following 1,000 years the Land Walls rendered Constantinople invulnerable to attack by successive waves of Hun, Slav, Arab, Persian, Avar and Bulgar invaders. The fortifications run for over 4 miles from the Sea of Marmara to the Golden Horn. Though now ruinous and covered in grass and wild flowers, they are still mightily impressive, composed of a chain of double walls, the inner one 12 yards high by 5 yards thick, connected by a wide terrace. The walls are further strengthened by 96 towers, and an impressively deep and wide moat.

One of the most noteworthy points of interest is the Golden Gate, near the Sea of Marmara, a Roman triumphal arch erected by Theodosius the Great in around AD 390. Byzantine emperors traditionally marked their investiture and celebrated their victories by entering the city through this gate, originally covered in gold plate. It forms part of the formidable Yedikule, known as the Castle of the Seven Towers, which, for many years, served as a prison.

Many ambassadors have been imprisoned in the tower by the entrance to the fortress, some of whom have carved their names and dates on the walls, with a litany of their sorrows. The most notable prisoner to be executed here was the 17-year-old

Osman II in 1622, who was probably mad, one of his crimes being the use of his pages for archery practice. After four years of misrule, his janissaries took appropriate revenge, strangling him with a bowstring. If you are of a gory disposition, and have the chance to make a visit, don't miss the 'well of blood', down which the heads of those executed are thrown before they are washed out to sea.

THE FALL OF CONSTANTINOPLE

In April 1453 Mehmet II, who had recently become sultan, and his army appeared before the Land Walls.

For seven weeks, despite a constant bombardment, and waves of attacks, the vastly outnumbered Byzantine and Genoese defenders held firm.

The Turks' most formidable weapon was a gigantic cannon, 8 yards long, cast by the renegade Hungarian Urban, and capable of firing a cannon ball for one mile.

On 29 May, Mehmet's elite troops, the janissaries, finally broke through the walls at their weakest point, where they run across the valley of the river Lycus.

Constantine XI, the last Byzantine emperor, and the Genoese commander Giustiniani were killed in the desperate fighting.

It is no wonder that Mehmet named himself the Conqueror after breaching these mighty walls.

THE KARIYE MOSQUE

If you want to go off the beaten track, one of the most beautiful small mosques in the city, formerly the church of St Saviour in Chora, is situated just inside the Land Walls. You may have met some Greeks in Istanbul who have talked about this building, one of the most beautiful creations of their ancestors. You will need to persevere to find the Kariye Mosque, but it is well worth it, especially if you have been impressed by the Byzantine mosaics in Ayasofya. The exterior, with its brick domes, is fairly simple, and gives little indication of the wealth within. The interior, even though it is encased in plaster and dirt, is quite extraordinary. The walls, and even some of the ceilings, are completely covered in mosaics and frescoes depicting the lives of Christ and the Virgin; if you can see beneath the dirt, you can only marvel at the skill of the mosaicists and fresco painters.

The mosaics were made for a local Byzantine patron of the arts called Theodore Metochites, a high-ranking Byzantine official at the beginning of the 14th century. The church survived the desperate fighting on the walls just a few yards away when the Turks broke into Constantinople in 1453, though its most famous possession, an icon thought to have been painted by St Luke himself, disappeared. It was a powerful eunuch at court called Atik Ali Pasha who converted the building into a mosque at the start of the 16th century.

THE RUSTEM PASHA MOSQUE

If you want to see what a top Ottoman official could achieve with the profits of office, visit the fascinating mosque commissioned by the fabulously rich Rustem Pasha, grand vizier to Suleyman the Magnificent. As you would expect, Rustem Pasha wanted only the best, and so employed the renowned Sinan as his architect. The mosque is unusual in its position, raised up above the shops in the labyrinth of streets surrounding the Spice Bazaar. It is easy to miss the unprepossessing entrance, tucked away above some straw-weavers' shops. The interior, in contrast, is quite dazzling, completely covered with the very finest blue, white and tomato red Iznik tiles. The decoration, with floral and geometric designs, covers every column, the mihrab, and even the facade.

Rustem Pasha, like so many of the most important officals, came from the Christian provinces of the Ottoman Empire. He was a Croatian who rose through the imperial ranks to serve Suleyman twice as grand vizier. His cleverest career move was to marry the Sultan's daughter Mihrimah Sultana in 1539. As he was widely seen as avaricious and venal, the match aroused great opposition, and his opponents spread the rumour that Rustem suffered from leprosy. In reply, the grand vizier summoned a doctor to check whether he had lice, known to be allergic to lepers. On being told by the doctor that he was, indeed, riddled with lice, Rustem was able to marry his princess.

While you are admiring the beauty of the mosque, it is perhaps best not to think of the lice-ridden man who commissioned it, a man who so hated poetry that Turkish poets of his time nicknamed him Minister Satan. Rustem Pasha spent his career feathering his own nest and, at his death in 1561, left behind vast estates, 1,700 slaves, 2,900 war horses and 1,106 camels.

THE CAGALOGLU BATHS

As we saw in Chapter 3, Turkish baths play a major part in the social life of Istanbul. Strange as it must seem to western Europeans, who must endure a bath a few times a year, the locals greatly enjoy their outings to the baths and attend several times a week. It is a social meeting point, a chance to do business, catch up on the news and exchange gossip, especially for women. The Cagaloglu Baths are housed in a beautiful building, and this is the place where you are most likely to see people of importance, if you can spot them in a state of undress through the clouds of steam. It stands midway between Ayasofya and the Grand Bazaar; more importantly, it is just round the corner from the Sublime Porte.

The baths themselves were built just nine years ago by Mahmud I, following a classic design that dates back to the baths of ancient Rome. It consists of identical sections for men and women, with hot and cooling rooms, bathing cubicles, and a steam room, where you sweat out all your impurities and are given a healthy massage, before bathing in the side chambers. After these exertions, you can return to the central room and relax with a cup of tea beneath the impressive dome. Running a bath is good business: the profits from Cagaloglu have paid for a new library to be installed in Ayasofya.

THE SULEYMANIYE

This superb mosque complex (*kulliye*) dominates the third hill of Istanbul, and is a worthy monument to Suleyman the Magnificent, the greatest of the Ottoman sultans. He is reputed to have spent 2½ million gold pieces on its construction. Fortunately, he was a very successful general and amassed enormous wealth from his military conquests, so he could afford it. The mosque was built by Sinan, his famous architect, between 1550 and 1557, and work continued on the surrounding buildings for some years afterwards. Interestingly, half the craftsmen who worked on the building of the mosque were Christians. Sinan spent his whole career attempting to surpass the grandeur of Ayasofya and it is interesting to compare the Suleymaniye, his finest work in Istanbul, with its great predecessor.

When visiting the mosque, you first cross the grand courtyard, with its columns of porphyry, marble and granite, and flanked by a great pylon, where the mosque astronomer lives. Like Ayasofya the vast interior is dominated by a lofty dome and semi-domes giving a sense of immense grandeur. It seems incredible that the weight of dome can be supported by the outer walls, but Sinan has cleverly hidden buttresses within them. The decoration is limited to stunning Iznik tiles, beautiful stained glass windows and inscriptions on the east wall.

Like other major mosques, the building is part of a great complex, a city in miniature comprising the mosque itself, two colleges on the precipitous

SINAN

Born a Christian, Koca Mimar Sinan (*c.* 1491–1588) served in the Janissaries as a military engineer before Suleyman appointed him chief of the imperial architects.

For 50 years he built on a prodigious scale, one of the most prolific architects who has ever lived – he built an incredible 131 mosques and 200 palaces, plus countless baths, schools, mausoleums, hospitals, aqueducts and bridges.

The fact that Sinan chose to be buried in the grounds of the Suleymaniye shows the attachment he felt for this building.

SULEYMAN THE MAGNIFICENT

During Suleyman's long reign (1520–66), the Ottoman Empire reached its greatest extent, from Algiers to the Crimea, and from the Persian Gulf to the plains of Hungary.

With his conquests came enormous wealth – Suleyman never wore the same clothes twice and ate off solid gold plate encrusted with jewels.

This splendour earned Suleyman the epithet 'the Magnificent' in the west; in Turkey, he is known as a wise law-giver.

Suleyman's harem consisted of 300 women, but the sultan was only interested in one.

This was the beautiful slave Haseki Hurrem, whom he named Roxelana when he took her as his wife.

Roxelana, lusting for power, persuaded her husband to execute his grand vizier Ibrahim Pasha and his eldest son and heir Mustafa, so that her own son could succeed.

Suleyman's reign was a great period for the arts, particularly architecture, Iznik ceramics and calligraphy.

My woman of the beautiful hair, my love of the slanted brows, my love of eyes full of mischief.

SULEYMAN WRITING TO HIS WIFE

---

north slope of the hill, two hospitals, one for mental patients, a bath, a han, stables and a soup kitchen. Some 700 people work here, their wages paid for from the income received from over 200 villages. Don't miss the tombs in a walled garden, including those of Suleyman and his wife Roxelana. Rather surprisingly, there is also a wrestling ground, a sport favoured by Turks because Mohammed was known to have been a keen wrestler (a Christian might find it difficult to imagine Jesus indulging in a little light-hearted wrestling with his Disciples!).

(Opposite) The imposing Suleymaniye is the architect Sinan's masterpiece; the Rustem Pasha Mosque can be seen in the foreground.

THE GALATA TOWER

If you are staying in Galata, you will certainly have noticed this tall watchtower, with its conical cap, which is the dominant landmark in this area. Once used by the Byzantines as an observation post to watch shipping on the Golden Horn, the present structure dates back to 1348 and was built by the Genoese, who dominated this part of Constantinople, where they had been awarded the status of most favoured trading nation. They named it the Tower of Christ, and made it the apex of the fortifications that defended their enclave. If you climb the 190-foot high tower, you can enjoy a wonderful view over the city and particularly

The Galata Tower is the dominant landmark in the European quarter of the city.

over the European quarter, which lies right at your feet. For any budding artist, this is far and away the best place to do a sketch of Istanbul, with the mosques and their minarets lining the skyline, and the Golden Horn in the foreground.

For a while after the conquest, the tower served as a prison before it was turned into a naval depot. An extraordinary event occurred here in the early 1630s. The writer Evliya Celebi, who wrote a memorable (though not always reliable) account of his travels throughout the Ottoman Empire a hundred years ago, records the amazing tale of an attempt to fly by Hezarfen Ahmed Celebi:

'First he practised by flying over the pulpit of Okmeydani eight or nine times with eagle wings, using the force of the wind. Then, as Sultan Murad Khan [Murad IV] was watching from the Sinan Pasha mansion at Sarayburnu, he flew from the very top of the Galata Tower and landed in the Dogancilar square in Uskudar, with the help of the southwest wind.' Although the Sultan was highly impressed, giving the aviator a sack of golden coins, he was also uneasy, commenting 'This is a scary man. He is capable of doing anything he wishes. It is not right to keep such people,' and promptly dispatching him to exile in Algeria. The locals all believe this tale implicitly, so don't express your reservations in public even if you regard it as no more than a tall story.

IX *Vanmour depicts the Dutch ambassador Cornelis Calkoen holding an audience with Sultan Ahmed III in Topkapi Sarayi, 1727.*

X (Opposite) *The sultan and his courtiers enjoying the beauties of Topkapi gardens.*

XI, XII (Above) *Calkoen and his entourage crossing the Second Court at Topkapi.* (Below) *A panoramic view of the extensive First Court.*

XIII (Left) *Women of the harem enjoying a walk in the gardens of Topkapi Sarayi.*

XIV (Below) *A European artist's impression of the comings and goings inside the harem – a never-ending source of intrigue.*

XV (Opposite) *The sultan's semi-naked concubines beautifying themselves in the baths of the harem; notice their extraordinary raised shoes.*

XVI (Opposite) *Dancing is a much-admired skill, as this young woman demonstrates.*

XVII (Below) *The whirling dervishes are one of the most remarkable sights in Istanbul – try to see them if you can.*

XVIII *Sultan Ahmet III watching tightrope walkers from a yali during a nautical festival on the Bosphorus.*

VII · TOPKAPI SARAYI

Topkapi Sarayi is in a most beautiful setting overlooking the Bosphorus. It has been the main seat of the sultans ever since Mehmet the Conqueror chose to locate his new palace there, over the original site of the ancient city of Byzantium. For any visitor to the city, Topkapi is a place of great fascination simply because access is so limited. It is possible to gain an impression of the buildings that house the sultan's court, but your main interest will undoubtedly focus on the inner sanctum that contains the harem, strictly out of bounds. The name of the palace gives an idea of its dual function: *topkapi* means 'cannon gate', an appropriate name for the founder of the palace who had employed a giant cannon to blast his way through

the walls of Constantinople; *sarayi*, in contrast, is a corruption of the word seraglio (the women's quarters in a Muslim house). There are reputed to be 400 women in the current sultan's harem (out of a total of 4,000 people living in the palace), an extraordinary number to satisfy the needs of just one man, even if he is the Shadow of God upon Earth.

THE FIRST COURT

The palace becomes more secretive the further you progress and you can feel hidden eyes watching as you move from court to court. The layout essentially consists of four courts separated by high walls. The First Court, also known as the Court of the Janissaries, is a huge unpaved area open to all, though the 50 guards in the gateway, heavily armed with an array of scimitars and arquebuses, do nothing to make you feel welcome as you pass through.

Your first impression as you enter the First Court is one of silence, so intense that visitors do not even dare to cough. Even the horses tread more softly. Only the imperial band salutes can break the silence when they perform for one hour at dawn and dusk, and to mark

This view of Topkapi shows why the palace is renowned for enjoying the most beautiful position in the whole of Istanbul. Access to the inner courts is strictly controlled, and you will need your wits about you to visit.

the stiff formality of Ottoman ceremonial does not apply here. The patients are given free wine, and rumour has it that the sick even drink in front of the sultan, who is a frequent visitor.

the end of an ambassador's audience with the sultan.

In the centre of the court stand some fine plane trees, but, as so often in Topkapi, there is a sinister undertone. Normally, you can enjoy the picturesque sight of janissaries parading under the trees, but, just occasionally, you will see one of their number, guilty of some heinous crime, swinging from the branches. The janissaries are well aware of their unique status, and it is under these trees that they overturn their soup kettles as a sign of revolt, something that has happened all too often in recent years.

The buildings that overlook the court reflect its relatively minor position in the palace hierarchy. A long range on the right houses the hospital for pages of the palace school. This always seems to be suspiciously full, perhaps because

WAYS INTO THE PALACE

Above the main entrance through the Imperial Gate is a room reputedly used by the women of the harem to watch processions pass.

The niches flanking the doorway have a more sinister purpose: they are used to display the severed heads of disgraced dignitaries.

The most imposing entrance is through the Iron Gate – this is how officials and foreign dignitaries arriving by sea enter the palace.

Two imperial caiques are moored outside the Topkapi Gate. They are ready at a moment's notice should the sultan decide to set sail.

The gate is flanked by two square towers with two enormous cannons that are fired to announce important religious festivals.

The pantry is reputed to be stocked with items ranging from marmalade to poison, and even eunuch's urine, much sought after as an aphrodisiac.

Behind a blank wall alongside the hospital are the bakeries, placed well out of the way as they are notoriously liable to catch fire. These bakeries produce the finest white bread, which is much appreciated by the sultan and his favourites. Opposite the hospital stands the imposing Byzantine church of St Irene. This has long ceased to be an Orthodox place of worship, and is instead used to house an arsenal and the imperial mint. Goldsmiths are kept busy here making precious pieces of jewelry for the ladies of the harem.

Another 50 fierce-looking soldiers stand guard beneath the octagonal tower and conical top of the impressive gate ahead. If you have the temerity to speak, they will instantly command you to be silent. Anyone on horseback will be ordered in no uncertain fashion to dismount; only the sultan is allowed to ride through these hallowed portals. The Turks have named this entrance the Gate of Salutation, though it is also the site of executions. The victim is usually dispatched with a silken cord or bowstring but occasionally the chief executioner uses a sword, in which case he will wash the blood from the blade in the fountain to the right. Next to the gate are two stones where the severed heads of the victims are displayed, those above the rank of pasha ending up impaled on iron spikes above the gate, those of a lower class exposed in niches below.

THE SECOND COURT

On this sobering note you enter with some trepidation the Second Court, or the Court of the Divan, as it is more commonly known. You will need to concoct a story that you are on official business to gain access. There is a deceptive feel to this court. On first appearance it is an oasis of tranquillity, with ancient cypress trees, fountains and gazelles grazing on the lawns. But this is also home to prison cells where those who have offended the sultan languish. The most notable of these is called the Cage, where the younger brothers of the sultan are brought up in total isolation in rooms enclosed by walled-up doors and windows, tended by deaf mutes and women who have been forcibly sterilized. At least they are spared fratricide, which had been the universal custom on the accession of every sultan from the conquest until the beginning of the 17th century. Jean-Claude Flachat, a French merchant living in Istanbul, recorded a first-hand account by the chief black eunuch Haci Besir Aga. He gave a vivid impression of 'the prison of the Princes', and of its 'dismal

Never hath a more delightful residence been erected by the art of man.

EVLIYA CELEBI

appearance', and of the claustrophobic nature of its inmates' existence, their every move observed by the eunuchs who guard them.

Make sure you see the council chamber set under an imposing portico. This is where the divan, the supreme executive and judicial council of empire, was formerly held four times a week; it now takes place in the grand vizier's palace in the Sublime Porte. During the divan, the court would have been filled with 5,000 janissaries who would stand in total silence, an awe-inspiring sight. Round the walls of the divan are low

The Second Court, with the divan hall in the centre and the domes of the harem beyond.

couches covered with carpets; the grand vizier would sit in the middle, with the lords of council on either side. Directly above his head is a window with a grille so that the sultan could eavesdrop on his ministers. The rooms near the divan house the inner treasury, where tribute and taxes from all over the empire is used to pay officials and janissaries.

You can see a series of highly prominent chimneys flanking the Second Court. They belong to Topkapi's vast kitchens. Nobody really knows how much food is consumed in the palace, but one estimate is that 200 sheep are eaten daily, 100 head of lamb or kid, 40 of veal, 50 brace of geese, and hundreds of pigeons, chickens and guineafowl.

The sultan listens in to proceedings in the divan hall from behind a screen while the grand vizier presides.

In a year it is reckoned that as many as 30,000 oxen, 20,000 calves, 60,000 sheep, 16,000 lambs, 10,000 kids and 100,000 turkeys are eaten in Topkapi. The kitchens contain vats big enough to hold a man, where preserved beef is dried and salted, and huge cauldrons in which two or three sheep can be cooked together.

In 1732 the awestruck Italian Count Marsigli provided a list of the vast quantities of food consumed regularly: 'rice, sugar, peas, lentils, pepper, coffee, sena, macaroons, dates, saffron, honey, salt, plums in lemon juice, vinegar,

water melons, 199,000 hens, 780 cart-loads of snow, and tin for cooking pots and fodder and forage for horses.' Just as impressive is the way the food is organized, with individual kitchens for the sultan, the females in his family, the black eunuch, and other ranks down to the chief cup bearer.

Another building well worth inspecting contains the sultan's stables. All Turks love horses, and the sultans are no exception. The stables house several hundred prize steeds, and a collection of fantastically ornate saddles and bridles, adorned with exquisite jewels, which are brought out on ceremonial occasions. But be careful when you make your visit – just off the stables is a permanently locked door, constantly supervised by black eunuchs, which leads to the women's quarters, strictly out of bounds.

One of the strangest sights in this court are the halberdiers, servants who are obliged to wear two false curls that fall from their tall top hat over their eyes like blinkers to prevent them enjoying sight of the sultan's beauties when they deliver firewood to the harem.

THE THIRD COURT

Your best chance to enter the Third Court is if you attach yourself to the entourage of a foreign ambassador. This court is generally reserved for high officials and members of the palace school, and you will have to rely on gossip to describe what goes on in the reception rooms of the sultan, the harem and the quarters of the black eunuchs. The name of the entrance to the court is enough to fire your imagination. It is known as the Gate of Felicity or the Door of the White Eunuchs, and is supposed to possess a mystical power. As so often the doorway serves a dual purpose: it is where the sultan is proclaimed, but also where the bodies of luckless officials who have incurred his wrath are flung to the mob. You may see someone fortunate enough to gain admittance kissing the doorway before passing into the Third Court.

Those who have seen inside tell of the charming pavilions. Just inside the entrance stands the throne room, a small pavilion encrusted with precious marble and gold ornamentation, where the grand vizier reports to the sultan. More importantly, this is where foreign ambassadors are received, an awe-inspiring occasion.

The surrounding buildings are devoted to the more intimate aspects of the sultan's life. The palace school houses 300–400 youths who are trained to serve their master. They are highly educated, with a good knowledge of sport, court etiquette, literature and the Koran, and a fluency in Turkish, Persian and Arabic. Forty of the most able pages are chosen to attend to an individual aspect of the sultan's life, ranging from cleaning the royal bedchamber to looking after the sultan's sword. This striving for physical and mental excellence means that the best of the pages often go on to become ministers and grand viziers.

The largest complex of buildings houses the famous House of Felicity, which contains the sultan's own quarters, as well as the harem. You can form some idea of the layout of the rooms and the peculiar lifestyle of its inhabitants from the accounts of the few outsiders who have gained access to this inner sanctum. The main room in the sultan's quarters is the Royal Hall, where he enjoys the pleasures of his favourites, listening to musicians playing in a gallery, and enjoying his women singing and dancing. These rooms are said to be decorated with the finest tiles, and are filled with the soft sound of water falling from fountains in the garden outside.

Each sultan adds to the work of his predecessors. The last sultan, Ahmed III, constructed a library, and a dining room entirely covered with wooden panels decorated with fruit and flowers. In the latter, the sultan is said to dine alone off gold plates set with precious stones, seated on a carpet. He is attended to by a servant kneeling before him, his chief taster, dressed in red trousers, on hand to make sure his food has not been poisoned, and the chef attendant of the napkin nearby. Other servants such as the fruit-server,

Suleyman the Magnificent and his grand vizier in one of the pavilions that are such a delightful feature of Topkapi.

pickle-server and sherbet-maker are in attendance should the sultan want to taste their delicacies. Other servants are busy cutting up the meat so that it is in easily digestible small pieces, since no cutlery is used.

Beyond the Third Court there is a delightful, enclosed garden, filled with pleasure domes, enjoying magnificent views over the Bosphorus and the Golden Horn. Part of it is a tulip garden, much loved by Ahmed III, whose master of flowers planted thousands of bulbs in the form of an amphitheatre. During the April full moon the tulips were in full flower,

while above them glass balls containing liquids of different colours and cages of canaries and nightingales hung from the trees. The sultan was entertained by his harem, pretending to hold a bazaar in his honour, or he watched them indulging in a treasure hunt for sweets hidden in the grass.

Like his predecessor, Mahmud spends hours here, watching his concubines disporting themselves among the flowers, or having his mutes and buffoons row him up and down the little artificial lake. The French merchant Flachat recorded how the sultan would order the gates to be closed, whereupon his concubines, like 'a swarm of bees' would appear and display all their arts with 'the cleverest coquetry', indulging in games 'that the poets invented for Cupid and the nymphs'. When Mahmud finally made his choice, the chief stewardess of the harem would present the girl to him and he would throw her his handkerchief.

THE HAREM

[My guide] *pointed me to a grate in the wall, but made me a sign that he might not go thither himself. When I came to the grate the wall was very thick, and grated on both sides with iron very strongly, but through the grate I did see thirty of the Grand Signior's concubines that were playing with a ball in another court....*

They wore upon their head nothing but a little cap of cloth of gold, which did but cover the crown of the head; no bands about their necks, nor anything but fair chains of pearl and a jewel hanging on their breast, and jewels in their ears. Their coats were like a soldier's mandilion, some of red satin and some of blue and some of other colours; they wore breeches of scamatie, a fine cloth made of cotton wool, as white as snow and as fine as lawn, for I could discern the skin of their thighs through it. These breeches came down to their mid-leg; some of them did wear fine cordoban buskins, and some had their legs naked, with a gold ring on the small of their leg; on their feet a velvet pantoufle, four or five inches high. I stood so long looking upon them that he which had showed me all this kindness began to be very angry with me. He made a wry mouth and stamped his foot to make me give over looking the which I was very loth to do, for the sight did please me wondrous well.

THOMAS DALLAM, *DIARY*, 1599–1600
(DALLAM WAS THE CREATOR OF A
MAGNIFICENT ORGAN AND AUTOMATON,
A GIFT FROM ELIZABETH I TO MURAD III)

The harem (the word literally means forbidden), or seraglio, as it is also known, is a continual source of fascination to locals and foreigners alike. It remains a mythical place, full of fabled luxury and hidden delights. You may see a covered carriage emerge from the Carriage Gate, taking the sultan's beauties to one of his summer resorts, or catch a glimpse of the black eunuchs whose sole job is to keep guard, day and night.

Hundreds of women live in the harem, organized in a strict hierarchy. There are all sorts of exotic jobs to be done, under the supervision of the harem stewardess, distinguished by her fur-lined robe, jewelled headdress and silver mace, her badge of office. Beneath her are the mistress of ceremonies, who oversees births, weddings and circumcisions, the women in charge of the sultan's children, the mistress of the bathhouse, and the coiffeur mistress who is always a mute, so that she cannot reveal any secrets confided in her. At the centre of the harem, like a spider in her web, is the valide sultan, who is reputed to live in magnificent apartments, beautifully decorated with Iznik tiles, with furniture inlaid with mother-of-pearl and ivory, the floors spread with the finest Persian carpets.

At the bottom of the social ladder are the novices. These are girls who have been bought in the slave markets or kidnapped by brigands or pirates. Ottavio Bon, the Venetian ambassador who did manage to see their lodgings back in the 17th century, recorded how they slept in an extensive dormitory that could accommodate up to 100 girls. He wrote that they were under strict supervision, even at night, with an older woman looking after every ten girls, and lamps at night to prevent too much intimacy between the girls.

Bon also saw the rooms where the royal princes are still educated until they are eleven years old. They study religion, literature, Arabic and Persian, astronomy and sciences. As only one of these boys can become the next sultan, there is great jealousy and competition between their mothers. Not surprisingly, the sons of different mothers are brought up separately in case one of them should meet an 'accident'. Every care is taken over the boys' welfare, as Bon recorded when he visited the splendid hospital built for them, and saw the extraordinary range of drugs and spices in the dispensary, including ground unicorn horn and various antidotes to poison.

A sultan enjoys watching ladies of the harem dancing before him in the Topkapi gardens.

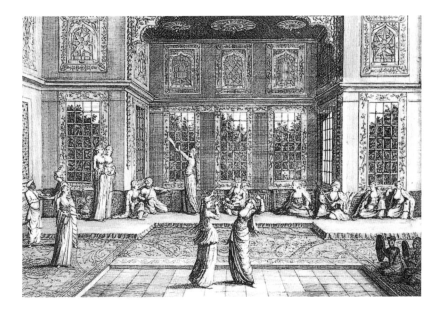

Dancing is regarded as a key attribute for ladies of the sultan's harem, and is no doubt a good way to attract the sultan's attention.

If the gossip is correct, the concubines who spend their lives in the harem are mostly Tatars, Circassians or Georgians, reputed to produce the most beautiful women, with the occasional negress to add an exotic element. On arrival at the Ottoman court they are immediately subjected to an intimate inspection by the eunuchs in case they suffer from any physical blemish. Once they have passed this test, they are taken to the valide sultan for approval. By now they will have become Muslims and been given a new name representing their character or attributes, and suggestive of beauty and physical desire. Typical examples are Little Swallow, Rose of Spring, Moon-Shaped One, Sugar Crystal or She Who Enamours the Heart.

TOKENS OF LOVE

Handkerchiefs are used in the harem for various purposes, including the wrapping up of fruit and gifts. The colour of the cloth used has special significance:

Red – passionate love

Pink – the bond of love

Purple – suffering from love

Orange – heartache

Green – intention

Blue – longed for union

Black – separation

THE CEREMONY OF TAKING COFFEE

This Turkish passion for coffee shows no sign of abating.

Five servants are involved under the control of the coffee stewardess:

The first brings in a brass tray, under which is placed a tiny brazier, scented with cedar wood.

The second pours rose water from a rock crystal ewer over the fingers of the sultan or his mother.

A third proffers a tiny napkin embroidered with pearls.

A fourth holds a small pot with the coffee and pours the precious beverage into a jewelled cup.

A fifth produces a tray on which are displayed a tempting array of pomegranates, apricots and figs on a bed of crystallized sugar rose petals.

Life is carried on at a slow pace since the sole object of the women's existence is to give pleasure to the sultan. In consequence, long hours are spent relaxing on divans, enjoying frequent cups of coffee, nibbling on fruit, cakes and sorbet, indulging in gossip and smoking hookahs. The concubines love sweet drinks, which they consume by dipping a large spoon into a communal crystal goblet. A particular favourite is sherbet, flavoured with lime, apple or violet, or the stronger flavours of musk, ambergris or aloe. Some of the more lascivious sultans are reputed to have instructed their servants to put opium into the drink, so that the favourite for the night

The girls now embark on a long period of training and live an existence similar to girls in a European seminary. They are taught to read and write in Turkish, to sew and embroider, and to learn attractive skills such as singing, dancing and making music. The most beautiful and sensual are sent to attend on the sultan's mother or his wives, where a close eye is kept on their progress, while those with lesser attributes become servants or governesses.

Making music is another attribute that concubines need to master.

would prove more amenable to their advances.

If you think that fantastic stories about these beauties are all figments of the imagination, then you must read the recent account of Jean-Claude Flachat, who recorded how Mahmud handed new chemises to his concubines when they went to the bath in the harem, but secretly ordered his tailors

Legend has it that dropping a handkerchief is how the sultan indicates his preferred nocturnal companion.

to remove all stitches, so the heat from the bath caused the glue to melt and they fell apart, leaving the girls naked. The sultan, who was watching from behind a screen, was much amused.

Many of the women are adept musicians, and entertain their fellow concubines on the lute, psaltery or lyre. As you would expect, many of them are also superb dancers. One Venetian diplomat, lucky enough to see some of them perform, commented that they were so sensual they would 'make marble melt'. When people discuss what these women really feel, spending their lives confined to the harem, opinion is divided. Some consider them little better than slaves but Lady Wortley Montagu, one of the few western women to meet some of the inmates, held a markedly different view. She thought the institution gave the sultan's concubines the chance to give free rein to their dreams, passions and thoughts.

EXOTIC TASTES IN THE HAREM

A Slave to your commands, Great Monarch, awaits your beckon, may she now be admitted?

AARON HILL ON A CONCUBINE'S
REQUEST TO THE SULTAN

The most intriguing aspect of the harem, of course, is what happens when one of the odalisques catches the sultan's eye, and there is much gossip on this subject. Great care is taken to ensure that she is in perfect physical condition to satisfy her lord's every desire. The lucky concubine is soaped and washed by slaves, her skin rubbed with cloves and ginger to increase her allure. When she has been washed and massaged, she is perfumed and dressed in sumptuous robes, and her hair covered in jewels. Thus attired she passes the black eunuchs on guard and enters the holy of holies in absolute silence. By the light of flickering torches she approaches the foot of the bed, modestly disrobes, lifts the bottom of the coverlet with her forehead, before advancing up the bed until she meets her master face to face. She is then free to apply all the skills she has learnt from her training in the harem.

The following morning the sultan presents her with a gift commensurate with the degree of satisfaction she has given. Occasionally, she will have performed poorly, in which case she risks ending up in the hands of the sultan's chief gardener and executioner who will put her in a weighted sack and drop her into the Bosphorus. It is much more likely, however, that she will have given satisfaction, and so will be officially installed as a favourite and treated with respect by servants and eunuchs. If she then becomes pregnant, her status will rise higher still, and, if the baby is a son, she may well be recognized as an official wife and showered with riches. Since her son may become the next sultan, she

must now use all her wiles to protect him. The stakes are enormously high, which is why there is such ferocious competition between the mothers, with rumours of cabbalism and necromancy being used to try to protect their precious offspring.

THE SULTAN'S OFFSPRING

If the sultan produces a child while you are in Istanbul, you will instantly know which sex it is, since the news is announced with a salvo fired from a cannon by the Topkapi Gate, seven for a boy, three for a girl, and this announcement is repeated five times over the following 24 hours. Within the palace the event is marked by the sacrifice of five rams for a boy, three for a girl, while locals take to the streets to celebrate, and processions of dignitaries make haste to deliver letters of congratulation.

A few days after the birth the happy mother is placed in a magnificent bed, where she will receive visits from the most important people at court, while a midwife and a wet nurse sit at the foot of the bed, the latter holding the precious baby. On the sixth day the baby, placed carefully in a new cradle, studded with jewels and adorned with feathers, is carried by the chief black eunuch into the harem, accompanied by ministers and court officials. The cradle is then filled with gold coins.

From the beginning, it is clear that there is no equality in status between the sultan's sons and daughters. They have very different roles to play. One of the sultan's sons will succeed him, and this idea rules their lives. The boys are taught archery, hunting, physical exercise, horsemanship and the use of arms. A boy's circumcision is a major occasion and there are reports by those who have witnessed it of the ornate ritual that surrounds the event. The royal prince is clad in scarlet and gold, with black heron's plumes nodding from his turban, and armed with a jewelled sword and a crystal-headed mace. After the operation, performed by a specialized barber with a sharpened razor, the wound cauterized with wood ash, the foreskin is sent in a golden cup to the prince's mother, and the knife to his grandmother. You will find more information about the festivals celebrating a royal circumcision in Chapter 9. Once the prince has recovered, he is often sent to serve in one of the provinces, usually Asian, far away from the temptations of Europe.

Royal princesses, on the other hand, enjoy a much closer relationship with their father. They are kept at court, where they learn to read and write, play music and sew embroidery. When they marry, it is to an Ottoman noble, never a foreign prince. The indulgent sultan gives a dowry consisting of property, expensive jewels and an extensive wardrobe. You will recognize these sultanas, as the royal princesses are known, by the small, sharp dagger, studded with precious stones, that

Roxelana was the favourite concubine and later wife of Suleyman the Magnificent; she was renowned for the level of influence that she had over her husband.

they wear attached to their belt. Their children are given royal rank but their sons are not allowed to hold a position at court, as this is thought to lead to factionalism. They are the only women in the Ottoman Empire with a rank superior to their husbands. This means that the husband of a sultana must ask permission from his wife before making sexual advances to her.

NOT AS OTHER MEN

The most powerful men in Topkapi are the eunuchs, and these men are the subject of much salacious gossip.

Their power is based on their constant access to the sultan and their control of the harem. The chief white eunuch is master of ceremonies, head gatekeeper, and head of the infirmary. Black eunuchs, in contrast, are restricted to the harem, and have been chosen for their ugliness and deformity to reduce the chances that one of the concubines will take a fancy to them. They are the guards who control all those entering and exiting the harem, accompany the concubines on excursions, and convey any messages they may want to send.

They also dispense justice to those who commit crimes within the inner sanctum, and are in charge of the education of the princes and princesses.

The head of the black eunuchs is a very powerful figure, dressed in a precious uniform adorned with fur. He controls the finances of the harem, as well as those of the imperial mosques in the city, receives rich endowments, and has 300 horses for his own personal use.

Owing to this power, and the fact that they are answerable to the sultan

The chief black eunuch holds a key post in the sultan's harem.

alone, eunuchs have acquired a sinister reputation, standing in the shadow of the sultan's throne, and watching his most intimate activities, with an eye pressed to the keyhole of the bedroom door.

You will often see eunuchs on the streets of Istanbul. They are an extraordinary sight, with beardless and wrinkled faces, fat, flabby bodies and long legs. Eunuchs tend to be effeminate, dressing with elegance, wearing perfume, and giving themselves names of flowers related to the women they guard. Some see them as being petulant, vindictive and arrogant, though others will tell you that they possess a strong vein of sentimentality, with a great fondness for children and animals. It is impossible not to feel pity at their terrible deformity, though some people feel nothing but revulsion.

Originally eunuchs were all white, but in the 16th century black eunuchs, mostly from Egypt, Sudan and Abyssinia, were introduced to the city, partly for their perceived ugliness and, more importantly, for their ability to survive the horrors of castration. It is a terrible operation, made worse by the fact that Islam forbids the practice. The operation has to be performed at one of the resting stations on the journey north, and by Jews or Christians, never Muslims. The death rate is high, particularly among the whites, which is why black eunuchs command such a high price. In fact not many come to the open market. Most are sold directly to the harem or to a wealthy potentate.

The actual operation consists of removing the penis, and either crushing or removing the testicles by bruising, twisting or searing. A tube is then put into the urethra. The wounds are cauterized with boiling oil. The risk of death is considerably less if the operation is carried out before puberty, but the psychological scars remain forever. If you ever have the chance to inspect a eunuch's turban, you may find inside it a pipe that he uses to help to urinate. Despite their terrible loss, many of them are still capable of sexual activity, with the help of aphrodisiacs and sexual aids. Ironically, the urine of eunuchs is itself regarded as a potent aphrodisiac.

The Patient [is put] into a Bath of warm Water, to soften and supple the Parts, and make them more tractable; some small time after, they pressed the Jugular Veins, which made the Party so stupid, and insensible, that he fell into a kind of Apoplexy, and then the action could be performed with scarce any Pain at all to the Patient.

CHARLES ANCILLON, *EUNUCHISM DISPLAY'D,* 1718

I am a witness to the fact that these black infidels are so traitorous that they may fall in love with one or two of the odalisques [female slaves] and spend all that they earn on them. At every opportunity they meet secretly and make love.

ALI SEYDI BEY, 18TH-CENTURY HISTORIAN

VIII · MUSLIMS, CHRISTIANS AND JEWS

Since Istanbul is a Muslim city it is advisable to learn the rudiments of Islam so that you do not offend the locals. There are five central pillars of Islam, as revealed to Mohammed by God through the archangel Gabriel: belief in one God and his Prophet Mohammed, praying five times a day (hence the regular call to prayer), giving alms to the poor, fasting during Ramadan, and going once in a lifetime on a pilgrimage to Mecca.

THE SULTAN AT PRAYER

The most magnificent and interesting [procession] I ever beheld. The rich and various costumes, the beauty and furniture of the Arabian horses, the comely appearance of the janissaries and royal corps of gardeners, in a word the splendour, the novelty, the silence and solemnity of this spectacle cannot I think but make a most powerful impression upon every foreign spectator.

THOMAS WATKINS, *A TOUR THROUGH SWITZERLAND TO CONSTANTINOPLE*

Every Friday the sultan emerges from Topkapi Sarayi to go to a mosque for midday prayers. You can easily find out which one if you ask anyone associated with Topkapi. This is an excellent chance for you to catch sight of him, and a very impressive sight it is, though the guards accompanying him hold poles with ostrich feathers round his head to hide his face from the crowds. A great deal of trouble is taken to ensure that the populace are impressed. On the Thursday night, the sultan's horse is suspended from straps so it walks through the streets with proper gravity the next day. It is a beautiful animal covered with a sumptuous coat embroidered with jewels.

A century ago the English adventurer George Sandys watched awestruck as the sultan passed by and wrote of the silence of the crowd, as if 'men were folded in sleep, and the World in midnight'. Lord Charlemont recently watched as fresh earth and water were strewn across the street 'to prevent the dust from being offensive'. On the sultan's right walks his head valet, carrying a waterproof in case the Grand Turk should get wet. He also has a pocket full of silver coins that he scatters among the crowd at an appropriate moment.

When the sultan dismounted in the courtyard of the mosque, Lord Charlemont was impressed by the servants who appeared instantly. 'One of them bore in his hands the Turban of State,' he observed, 'which was of a peculiar size and form and richly set with diamonds, and the other a footstool of rich brocade which he placed near the door of the mosque for the Grand Signor to alight upon.' Having dismounted, the sultan performs his ablutions in the same way as his subjects for he believes, like all true Muslims, that water provides the path to paradise. He then proceeds inside the mosque, where he listens attentively while the imam reads from the Koran, standing to the left of the mihrab.

The current sultan is known to be a religious man and he pays particular attention to celebrating the birthday of Mohammed. Panegyrics of the Prophet are proclaimed on this important day at three of the imperial

The sultan's procession to a mosque for Friday prayers is your best chance to see him.

The Janissaries line the street from the palace to the mosque; they are without any sort of arms; they stand with their hands across and bow down to the Grand Signior and to the vizier only; they return the salute.

LORD BALTIMORE

mosques, while a nativity ode is sung before the sultan who is then presented with a letter from the Sharif of Mecca (the traditional steward of the holy Muslim city), together with aloes and essence of roses.

MOSQUES

You can scarcely fail to notice the plethora of mosques all over the city. Their domes and minarets dominate the Istanbul skyline. You will find a wonderful feeling of space in the great mosques, which have domes seeming to float effortlessly above the worshippers. There is enough room to contain the population of a particular quarter and there is no furniture to obstruct the faithful's prostrations. The design of a mosque follows a set format, and the walls are commonly adorned with tiles, but no

The Blue Mosque is named after the thousands of blue tiles that cover the walls of its interior.

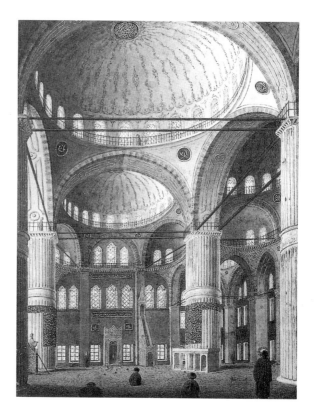

statues or paintings of human figures or animals are permitted since Islam forbids representations of living creatures. Rugs and carpets cover the floor while oil lamps are suspended on great chains.

The central feature is the mihrab, an ornate niche facing Mecca, with a lofty marble pulpit called a minbar beside it from where the imam delivers a sermon, often no more than a series of quotations from the Koran, during Friday prayers. Grander mosques also contain a raised platform from where the muezzin chants responses to the imam's prayers, which he may deliver from a sort of throne, known as the *kursu*. Mosques that are frequented by the sultan have a screened off balcony, where he can pray in safety. A wooden screen lattice at the back hides female worshippers.

The mosque is set within a courtyard, with flowing water, normally

I bear witness that there is no God but God, and I testify that Mohammed is his Prophet.

CALL FROM THE MUEZZIN

Muslims at prayer.

value, retaining a hereditary lease, and becoming a fixed tenant.

Every mosque has a minaret from which a muezzin chants five times a day. This call to prayer normally consists of phrases such as 'God is most great', and 'There is no God but Allah'. Not all visitors are impressed; Lady Craven complained of the 'bawling and hallooing to all good Musselmen'.

MUFTIS AND IMAMS

He [the mufti] *is possessed of absolute power in matters of religion. Affairs of state derive from religion; religion is the root, the state, the branch.*
ANONYMOUS 17TH-CENTURY QUOTATION

from a central fountain, where believers wash their head, hands and feet before going inside. The more popular ones have stalls where religious objects are sold. You might also see a letter-writer sitting on a low stool, his pen at the ready to draw up a contract or draft a petition, while a beggar waits patiently by the gateway.

The larger mosques, which serve as charitable foundations as well as places of worship, are invariably surrounded by a whole complex of buildings: a han to accommodate travellers, a kitchen, a hospital, and a college or *medrese*, usually recognizable from its row of small domes. Often there is a library nearby. Some of these complexes date back to the conquest in 1453 when large tracts of land were given to the mosques and their dependencies. In addition, they were generously endowed by the sultans, grand viziers and their families. There is also a tax advantage for a Muslim or, indeed, a Christian citizen to sell his land to a mosque for a fraction of its real

Although the sultan is caliph, there are a number of occasions when he defers to the Sheikh ul Islam, who is head of the clergy in Istanbul. It is the Sheikh ul Islam who expounds the Koran and the Sharia, or sacred Islamic law. He also controls scholars who have graduated from the medrese. You can easily recognize him and his senior clergy from their brightly coloured caftans and tall, white turbans, and by their carriages, which are draped in green. Below him there are large numbers of lesser clergy, including imams who deliver sermons and lead prayers. The larger mosques also employ, among others, doorkeepers, lesson readers and supervisors of ablutions. There is also the important mosque astronomer, who regulates prayers five times a day, announces the times of sunrise and sunset, often using a water clock or sundial, and determines the date of the lunar month from the first appearance of the sickle moon.

PIOUS FOUNDATIONS

One of the most attractive sides to Istanbul society are the pious foundations, known as *vakifs*, which are dedicated to the well-being and material welfare of the inhabitants of the city. They are endowed by rich men and women who give a donation, known as a *waqf*. The money is used for charitable purposes, paying for the upkeep of mosques, schools, hospitals and hans. Sometimes the donation is more modest, covering, for example, the provision of a drinking fountain. Craftsmen work in the ateliers of these foundations, and sell goods in the shops and markets they own. Merchants use their hans and shops, and drink in their coffee houses.

Vatifs also provide dowries for orphan girls and clothes for the needy, repay debts of those in prison, and give out food to the poor. It has been estimated that some 30,000 locals are fed daily by these institutions. The good work they do may account for the fact that there are not many beggars on the streets. If there is a natural disaster, such as an earthquake or a fire, the foundations provide money for the relief of stricken families and help to organize the reconstruction needed in the aftermath of the devastation.

However, if you talk to someone in government they may not be quite so complimentary about this apparent altruism. Money paid to them is non-taxable, as it is deemed to be for charitable purposes, and there have been a number of cases of embezzlement, where the directors of the vakif have quietly pocketed the money they are meant to be distributing. There is little the unfortunate donors can do, though they sometimes insert prayers into their deeds, putting their faith in God. On discovering one recent case of embezzlement, the donor altered his prayer to read 'May they be cursed by God, the angels and the people.'

They pray with Fervour and a fix'd Attention, never turning like too many Inconsiderate Christians in our Noisy Churches, to behold people pass behind them; all is still, and softly sacred... no opening Pews and Shutting them again, disturb the Congregation with their needless Clamour: no Holy-Talking, and Conceited Hypocrite outruns the Parson with her zealous Lips, while her lew'd Eyes, behind a Fan, are laughing heartily at some poor Jest her Ears have listen'd to.

AARON HILL

COLLEGES AND LIBRARIES

The most important centre for education is the medrese, the college attached to a mosque. This is where male students are given a traditional Muslim education based on 10 key subjects, including grammar, syntax, logic, philosophy, geometry, astronomy and calligraphy. The more advanced colleges teach sciences connected to the Sharia, including law, theology, rhetoric and jurisprudence. This will give successful students the training to become an imam, or judge.

Some of the medreses are built on a massive scale; the one beside the Fatih Mosque provides lodging for 1,000 students. Its library contains 1,770 books, of which half were donated when it was originally set up by Mehmet the Conqueror. If you gain access to a library, you will see students sitting cross-legged on the matting carefully transcribing ancient texts. The main university in Istanbul is based off Beyazit Square, housing major faculties of theology, philosophy, law, medicine and science.

You will notice, as you travel through the city, that a large number of the few books you will see have been imported from abroad. For hundreds of years, there was a ban on printing them, since they were regarded as subversive by the clergy. This has only been lifted relatively recently. During the last sultan's reign an enterprising Transylvanian called Ibrahim Muteferrika persuaded the government to lift the ban and he was soon producing dictionaries, grammars and history books, though he was careful to print nothing

connected with Islam, knowing of the strong clerical opposition to printing. However, since his death in 1745, few books have been printed, and the scribes and calligraphers, who had feared that they would be put out of business, have resumed their work.

With a dearth of printed books, Turks became experts in the art of calligraphy, and you will find scribes seated on street corners writing letters in a beautiful hand for their illiterate compatriots. Some of the best examples are of the imperial monogram, known as the *tugra*. Popular designs show calligraphy in the shape of animals and birds. There is a saying, which is certainly believed, that 'The Koran was revealed in Mecca, recited in Egypt and written in Istanbul.'

The Ottomans love calligraphy and a scribe is an important figure.

This tugra of Suleyman the Magnificent is a veritable work of art. Simpler versions are used to sign official documents.

DEATH AND FUNERALS

You are unlikely to witness the death of a Muslim, but it is interesting to know how the locals behave. They are, by nature, fatalists, and believe that their actions, including their death, have been predestined by Allah. Dying men and women therefore accept their fate with resignation. As death approaches, loved ones recite from the Koran. Meanwhile, one of the family perfumes the bedchamber. After death the corpse is washed and the local imam rubs powdered camphor on the eight parts of the body that come into contact with the ground most frequently during prayer: the knees, hands, feet, nose and forehead. The nails and hair are trimmed, and then the body is wrapped in a long and seamless sheet, and the bier fumigated.

Muslims believe that the dead suffer torments before burial, therefore they are interred as quickly as possible, ideally before sunset on the day of death or early on the following day. The imam recites prayers over the bier, and the body is placed in the ground, with its right side turned towards Mecca. The chief mourner casts a handful of earth in, and then the imam says a brief funeral prayer and calls aloud three times the name of the deceased and his mother.

Tombs vary greatly. Richer families honour the deceased with an incredibly ornate tomb, consisting of slabs of marble, open in the centre and raised up, with a gable-shaped wooden frame placed over the top. The catafalque is shrouded by a black or green pall, embroidered with gold or silver thread, surrounded by a balustrade, and guarded by large candlesticks. Most tombs are considerably less ornate, normally consisting of two upright stones, one at the head, the other at the foot, with depictions of turbans for a man, lotus leaves for a woman. The Turks believe that providing earthly pleasures will delight the souls of the departed, so you may come across graves with offerings of money or meat, or sometimes with a marble trough where flowers grow. Occasionally they are covered with trellis cages housing songbirds, which bring comfort to the dead, it is believed.

Do good and throw it into the sea, even if the fish don't understand, God will know.

TURKISH PROVERB

[119]

An Ottoman funeral is taken with the utmost seriousness; here a crowd of mourners follows the funeral bier.

Muslims believe implicitly in hell, purgatory and paradise. When they are summoned from purgatory at the Last Judgment they must endure a tortuous journey, in which they must walk over a red-hot gridiron. This is why Muslims fervently believe that all paper that they have not trampled on will adhere to feet and stop them getting burnt. They must then pass over a bridge, in the words of the Swedish traveller Monsieur d'Ohsson, 'finer than a hair and sharper than a sabre: the elect will pass over it with the velocity of the wind, with the quickness of lightning; but the reprobates will slide off, and be precipitated into the midst of eternal fire'.

Alas, alas! Here free from
Cares and Strife,
Lies one embrac'd to death
by his first Wife;
Had'st thou been sow'r as
Persian Limons are,
Thou had'st not met a Fate
so sharp, so rare;
But as thou wast an Orange
thou art dead,
For Women love such
Sweetness, ev'n in Bed;
And she who by thee chanc'd
that Night to lie,
Tasted thee, found thee sweet,
and quickly suck'd thee dry.

AARON HILL RECORDING
AN ORANGE-SELLER'S DEATH
ON HIS WEDDING NIGHT

EYUP AND PLACES OF PILGRIMAGE

They lifted the stone and found below it the body of Eyup wrapt in a saffron-coloured shroud with a brazen play ball in his hand, fresh and well preserved.

EVLIYA CELEBI

The holiest part of the city for all Muslims is the suburb of Eyup, far up the southern shore of the Golden Horn. This is where the close companion and standard-bearer of Mohammed, Eyup Ansari, is buried, having fallen before the walls of Constantinople during the great Arab siege of 669. Pious Muslims like to make a pilgrimage to his tomb, often on his feast day, where they will light candles and make vows. Pilgrims believe that if they drink water from the cistern beside the tomb they will be cured of their afflictions. The tomb itself contains the horse of Mohammed II, reputed to have the power to cure crippled children.

A new sultan visits the tomb of Eyup on his accession, a ritual that has remained unchanged for centuries. He is the caliph, head of all Sunni Muslims and guardian of Mecca and Medina, the two holiest sites in the whole of Islam. He is also the possessor of the holy mantle of the Prophet, brought back from Egypt by Selim I in 1517. The sultan's visit to Eyup's tomb demonstrates his link with the Prophet. On arrival, normally by boat, he is girded with the sword of Osman, founder of the dynasty, by the chief of the Mevlevi dervishes, in

A view of Eyup, the holiest part of Istanbul for all Muslims.

the courtyard of the adjoining Sultan Mosque. He is then presented with offerings of incense, aloes, silver and gold. The return journey is normally by horseback, and the sultan will visit the tombs of his most eminent ancestors, starting with that of Mehmet the Conqueror, also in Eyup.

Very few non-Muslims live in Eyup, and those that do are strictly prohibited from opening a shop here. If you are brave enough to venture into the mosque, you can admire the beauty of the courtyard. The best time to visit is in spring, when the majestic plane trees are coming into leaf. Storks love

to nest in their branches. The graveyard, like so many in Eyup, is filled with flowers. But be aware that this is a strictly Muslim district, so pay due respect to local customs. You will find few Christians here.

An even more important pilgrimage is the one to Mecca, known as the *haj*, since, as one of the pillars of Islam, all Muslims aim to do this once in their lifetime. The initial point of departure is traditionally Topkapi, but for most people it is from Uskudar, on the Asian bank of the Bosphorus, 14 days before the Feast of Bairam. It is one of the major dates in the Ottoman calendar and a great sight. The cavalcade sets off with a camel at its centre bearing a precious black cloth covered with gold embroidery, a gift from the sultan to Mecca, where it will be placed over the sacred Kaaba. It is escorted by a vast crowd including officials, guards, dervishes and perfume sprinklers. Horsemen show off their skills with feats of swordsmanship, accompanied by tambourine players and dancers, to the delight of the spectators.

One of the strangest sights are the holy men who are inspired to make the pilgrimage. Some are naked, others 'dressed in a most fantastical manner', as Lord Charlemont observed, and yet others have snakes twined round their bodies, though some cynics regard them as opportunists looking for any chance to rob pilgrims in the caravan. If you see someone wearing a green turban, you will know that he has completed the pilgrimage already.

RAMADAN AND OTHER RELIGIOUS FEASTS

Ramadan is the most important religious festival in the Muslim calendar. It dates back to the time of Mohammed, who proclaimed that this was the moment when the gates of paradise were open, the doors of hell closed and the devil chained by one leg. Each day during the festival, which lasts a whole month (the dates change from year to year – see Chapter 1), no Muslim may eat, drink or smoke tobacco between sunrise and sunset, with the exception of the sick and travellers. The end of each day's fast at sunset is a time of high excitement. The moment that the sun vanishes is marked by the thunder of the cannon, accompanied by the roll of drums. Afterwards, every believer can happily devour their evening meal.

In the streets during Ramadan, outside the houses of leading Muslims, crowds gather to listen to preachers reciting from the Koran. Some owners set up tables outside their door from which they will dispense food to the poor, as well as to dervishes and holy men, who are welcomed into all Muslims' houses. At the most important mosques verses of the holy book are strung between the minarets in letters of fire. Two hours after sunset prayers are performed in the mosques.

A Turkish pilgrim enjoys a pipe as he embarks upon his journey.

Those who are guilty of misdemeanours during Ramadan are treated with the utmost severity. It has been known for a drunk in the streets to be compelled to melt a ladle of lead which is then poured down his throat.

On the 15th day, within Topkapi Sarayi, the sultan's family and senior members of the government are admitted to the Pavilion of the Holy Mantle, where the sacred raiment has been washed with rose water by the sultan's pages. They are then solemnly given a piece of paper engraved with the seal of the Prophet, which they dip into the rose water and swallow.

During Ramadan the gardens of the major mosques are turned into markets with pedlars selling their wares to the milling crowds. Beggars work the throng, their numbers increased since they know that Muslims have a duty to give to the poor. The poor go from one spectacle to another, eating as much food as they can. Tradesmen cash in on the opportunity too; there are even shops in the graveyards.

On the 27th day of Ramadan Muslims believe that they are celebrating the moment when the Archangel Gabriel revealed the contents of the Koran to Mohammed. This is a holy occasion, when all creation bows before Allah, and angels learn of the destinies of men. When Ramadan finally ends, at the appearance of the new moon, Muslims partake in the sugar festival, one of the most joyful moments of the year, three days of general merrymaking, when everyone gorges themselves on sweets and drinks. If you go to Okmeydan you will see all sorts of athletic contests, feats of archery, javelin throwing and bouts of wrestling.

Another important festival is the four-day Feast of the Sacrifice, known as Kurban Bayrami, shortly after Ramadan, where the head of every household has a duty to sacrifice a ram. Just before the festival the Beyazit Mosque resounds to the plaintive bleating of hundreds of sheep awaiting their fate, brought into the city by nomad shepherds. You will see families taking back their intended victim, its fleece stained with henna, and its horns covered with gold or silver leaf. It is traditional for the sultan and all well-off families to divide the sheep's flesh, one third for the household, one third for relatives and the final portion for the poor.

Muslims believe that the sacrificed sheep carries true believers over the bridge that leads to paradise. A great many of the sacrifices take place in the suburb of Eyup since it is home to so many important Muslim shrines, and this has led to the locals acquiring the nickname 'sacrificers'. During the festival presents are lavishly given, particularly to children, and you will see stalls outside mosques selling sweets and toys. Remember that, even though you are not a Muslim, this is a time when everyone is expected to dispense coins to the poor and the needy.

DERVISHES AND HOLY MEN

*On their heads they wore caps of the
same colour, usually made of camel's
hair, and, stiffened into the form of a
sugar loaf.*

LORD CHARLEMONT

The dervishes are a very popular religious group. Bearing a superficial
resemblance to monks in Western
Europe, they disregard many Islamic
conventions and do not mind if women
go unveiled. They are Sufis, unlike the
state religion, which is Sunni, and
enjoy a curious position in Turkish
society. They are much respected and
it is the *Chelebi*, the head of one of the
branches of the dervishes, who has the
great privilege of investing each new
sultan in the mosque at Eyup. And

you will find that many Muslims visit
tombs of leading dervishes, looking for
a cure to their ailments or praying for
the safe birth of a child.

There are two main groups: the
Mevlevis and the Bektashis (com-
parable to the Dominicans and
Benedictines in the Roman Catholic
church). The latter are particularly
popular, especially among the janissaries, a major reason being that drinking
of wine and spirits is permitted, and
women participate unveiled. The
Mevlevis are more commonly known
as the whirling or dancing dervishes
on account of the extraordinary rites
they perform every Friday. You should
try to go to one of their religious
centres and see the dervishes dancing;
it is an incredible sight. There is the
bonus that this is also one of the very

*The whirling
dervishes wear a
highly distinctive
costume.*

few ceremonies that Turkish women are allowed to attend, so it will give you an excuse to study them. Since the dervishes believe in austerity, there is no minaret outside their places of worship and the interior of a dervish mosque is normally no more than a bare room. You can show your appreciation of their life of simplicity by bringing an offering, which will symbolize the food brought by Gabriel to Adam after his expulsion from Paradise.

The whirling dervishes themselves are a remarkable sight, clothed in coarse, brown robes, which hang down to their feet and are fastened at the waist with a leather strap. On their heads they wear caps made of camel hair. At first they stand motionless while faint and melodious music begins, emanating from a sort of flute and kettledrum at the back of the hall. Gradually they start to twirl, their arms outstretched, the music getting louder and faster. The spiralling motion of their bodies goes faster and faster, their robes spreading as they dance, until they resemble the petals of a gigantic flower. The dancers appear as if in a trance, a serene expression on their faces, and without a trace of giddiness. They end their dance with the cry 'There is no God but God.' Dervishes believe that Mevleva, founder of the order, danced without pause for 15 days, after which

The gory sight of a howling dervish cutting himself, a truly barbaric act.

he fell into an ecstasy, and received from heaven the rule of the order. After the music dies away, the dancers retire with solemn gravity,

In contrast, the howling dervishes, based in Scutari in Asia, have a barbaric ritual, torturing themselves by placing red-hot irons in their mouths, or driving them into their arms and legs. Their aim, like that of the whirling dervishes, is to fall into an ecstasy that will allow them a vision of heaven.

Istanbul is full of holy men who come in different guises. Some dedicate themselves to the poor, and you will find coloured rags tied to their tombs and to those of other holy men by ardent believers looking for a blessing. Others appear much wilder, wandering through the streets completely naked, carrying heavy staffs.

These hermits and fakirs are much venerated by Muslims, who regard them as miracle workers and magicians. Travellers who are setting off on a journey often invoke their blessing. In earlier times they used to accompany the Turkish army into battle, and would often lead the charge against the enemy in the certain knowledge that their martyrdom for the faith would lead them straight to paradise.

RELICS AND SUPERSTITIONS

The Turks are a superstitious race, and this affects every aspect of their lives. They believe in the divination of dreams and even more strongly in the Evil Eye. To counter its baleful influence many people wear charms, the most popular being blue beads or glass balls, which they regard as an antidote; poorer Muslims are equally superstitious, wrapping chickpeas in blue cloth. So deep is this superstition that babies sometimes have a blue glass bead pinned to their dresses. The Turks are also afraid that Europeans with blue eyes will bring bad luck, so be prepared for strange looks if this applies to you.

Holy places in the city attract the superstitious too, notably the Sehzade Mosque on the third hill. It is very popular with barren, Muslim women and if you go there at noon on a Friday you will see the outer courtyard full of them. At the first note of the muezzin, they run as fast as they can to the minaret at the northeastern corner of the building. They believe that the first woman to touch it will be healed of her affliction, and, if she succeeds in becoming pregnant, she will give the other women a piece of cake in the belief that one of the seeds will enter their womb. A less attractive superstition is the belief that if you urinate on sugar which is added to a cup of coffee and given to the person you wish to attract, it will have an instant effect. Conversely, if you wish to destroy relations between a man and his wife, smear pig fat onto his clothes.

Muslims are even more superstitious about death. Bushes and foliage around the graves of saints are covered in scraps and rags of clothing which pilgrims tear from garments in belief that they will preserve them from sickness and misfortune. Even the birds that you will see everywhere in Istanbul are seen as symbolic: turtle doves represent love, swallows' nests protect your house from fire, and storks bring good fortune since they are thought to migrate annually to Mecca.

There is a very strong cult of relics in the city. Many of the most precious are kept in Topkapi Sarayi. They include a piece of the Prophet's tooth, hair from his beard, a footprint in marble from his right foot, and his cloak. Once a year, on the anniversary of the Prophet's birth, the ladies of the harem in their veils slowly file past these relics and kiss them. The sultan then presents them with handkerchiefs on which verses of the Koran have been embroidered.

Many of the most famous relics in the city date back to Byzantine times. They included the Virgin's robe (you can still find a relic of her girdle in the church of St Mary Chalcoprateia), the spear that pierced Christ's side as well as the sponge offered to him, the table from the Last Supper and the doors of Noah's Ark. Most of these objects disappeared after the conquest in 1453 but you will still find that many people believe that relics survive throughout the city. Beneath the Column of Constantine, so it is said, is buried Noah's hatchet, the baskets and rather stale remains of loaves which Christ fed to the multitude, the nails of his Passion and pieces of the True Cross. Locals put their complete faith in these relics; the figure of victory on the base of the Column of Marcian, for example, is reputed to be able to tell true from false virgins. Before setting off on the pilgrimage to Mecca, pilgrims place offerings on the sacred stone at Besiktas in Uskudar on which Jesus was said to have been washed after his birth.

One of the great unsolved mysteries of Byzantium is what happened to Constantine XI, the last emperor. He was seen fighting valiantly to repel the overwhelming hordes of Turkish troops pouring through the breach in the walls, but then was lost. However, if you visit the Gul Mosque beside the Holy Gate, or Aya Kapi, on the Golden Horn, and meet a local Greek, you will find that he or she has a very interesting story to tell. The Greeks believe that the Gul Mosque stands on the site of the church of St Theodosia, and that the body of the emperor was brought here in 1453 and buried in a chamber within the southeast pier of the church. The Turks, in contrast, and perhaps in a deliberate attempt to prevent the site becoming a place of pilgrimage, maintain that this chamber contains the remains of Gul Baba, founder of the mosque.

OTHER RELIGIONS

Islam is the dominant, but by no means the only, religion in Istanbul. It is reckoned by some that nearly half the population in the city are non-Muslims. They include the indigenous Greeks, and Italians and other nationalities who had settled here before the conquest, but also Jews who had fled European states that had persecuted them, notably Spain (a form of Castilian known as Ladino is used in some religious services), and Christians who came here to make money.

The most important of these religions is the Greek Orthodox, whose patriarch, once the rival of the pope himself, is installed in an anonymous-looking wooden building beside the simple church of St George (after the conquest in 1453 the Greeks were forbidden to build churches with domes or masonry roofs) in the Greek suburb of Phanar. The interior is rather more impressive, with a fine 16th-century patriarchal throne. Nevertheless, it is difficult to believe that it is from such a modest building that the patriarch continues to dictate the religious affairs of Eastern Christendom. The Greeks celebrate all sorts of festivals. One of the most memorable is in the church of Our Lady of the Fish at Balikli, which originated when a monk back in 1453, doubtful that Constantinople had fallen to the Turks, was convinced when the fish he was frying leapt out of the frying pan. Greek pilgrims, believing that the well where the fish live has miraculous powers, come here to seek a cure for their diseases; women also come to pray for a child.

Although the Greeks, in general, get on well with Muslims, that is less true of their relations with Jews. It is said that if a Jew appears in certain Greek neighbourhoods during Holy Week he will have his beard greased with tar and set on fire. The figure of a rabbi during Good Friday processions is subject to much abuse, and Jews are associated with Judas, who betrayed Christ; Easter eggs eaten during the procession are meant to celebrate his death.

In contrast, Jews enjoy good relations with Muslims though there are limits. They believe that if anybody, even a Muslim, steps over or under a coffin, they will be instantly transformed into a witch or a devil. Despite

The Armenian religion is very ancient; their priests wear wonderfully ornate vestments.

this religious handicap, the government renewed the *firman* (a royal decree) allowing the Jews to construct synagogues just six years ago. Little advantage has been taken of this, however, because the financial power of the Jews, once such a feature of life in Istanbul, has been largely replaced by that of the Armenians. The Armenian patriarch, although a lesser figure than his Greek counterpart, wields enormous power over his flock, and controls not only their churches but also their schools and printing presses.

The areas of Galata and Pera, where you are likely to spend much of your time, are dominated by Protestants and Catholics. If you are there on Easter Sunday, you will see the ambassadors, escorted by members of their households, riding through the streets to church with great pomp and ceremony.

IX · FESTIVALS, FIREWORKS AND TRIPS UP THE BOSPHORUS

THE SULTAN TAKES TO THE WATER

A trip up the Bosphorus will be one of the real delights of your stay in Istanbul. Every year dozens of new yalis appear on its banks, beautiful wooden mansions with stone bases, with gardens spreading up the hillsides behind. They are particularly beautiful in spring, when they are a riot of jasmine, honeysuckle and bougainvillea, and the judas and cherry trees are in blossom.

The sultan, like his subjects, likes to take to the water. He is keen to leave the city during the summer months and,

to acknowledge this, the government has officially decreed the date of 5 May as the beginning of the season, with 7 October allocated as the date to return to the city. Mahmud has recently built a new palace at Mahbubiye.

Don't miss the chance to see the sultan proceeding up the Bosphorus, seated under a silken canopy on the raised poop of a caique painted in scarlet and gold. You will be made aware of the approach of the sultan's boat by the strange sound made by his oarsmen, dressed in red caps with blue tassels, and white muslin shirts and breeches, who bark like dogs so

that nobody can overhear his conversation should he deign to speak. These oarsmen also serve as imperial gardeners, and are an elite unit.

As soon as his caique appears, all other craft on the water take cover.

If the sultan is leaving Topkapi for a while, his caique shoots through the water accompanied by a veritable fleet of barges and other boats, carrying members of the palace guard, high officials, and a bevy of beauties from the harem. The most entertaining sight is that of dwarves and mutes in brilliant silk robes, wearing curved swords, some with hunting dogs. The barges at the rear of the convoy are piled high with furnishings.

Although these outings seem to be devoted purely to pleasure, the sultan is taking no chances. He knows that the amount of time his predecessor spent outside the city meant that he lost touch with what was going on. Consequently, Mahmud's official summer residence at Besitkas is situated near Topkapi, so that he can return at a moment's notice to deal swiftly with any sign of fire or uprising. Sometimes, he goes out to visit a yali belonging to one of his nobles. Banquets, receptions and other entertainments, including sports competitions, music, poetry readings and walks in the gardens, are laid on.

*Had your father married
you off to a grandee*

*Thanks to you, we too could
move into a yali.*

ANONYMOUS POET

*These slender and elegant caiques are some
of the most beautiful boats on the Bosphorus.
No trip to Istanbul would be complete
without a trip on one.*

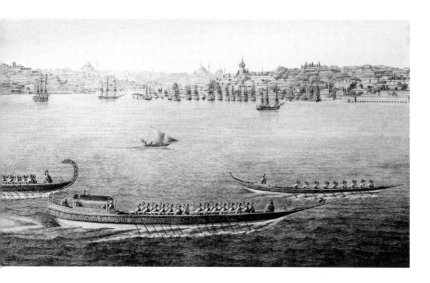

PLEASURE SPOTS

Yalis on the Bosphorus tend to look relatively modest on the outside, but the interiors are a different matter. If you are invited into one, you will be amazed at the sumptuous decoration. The reception halls are covered in carpets and have a divan round the walls. Often the walls, windows and even the ceiling are covered in floral and other motifs, with niches in the walls filled with flowers. Off this hall there are rooms on three sides, the fourth side projecting over the water. The building has broad and extensive fenestration to let in the maximum amount of light, with large openings all around. Not only can the owners look out, but passersby can also look in at the opulently decorated interiors.

Lady Wortley Montagu was much taken with the beauty of the yali she visited, particularly the 'profusion of marble, gilding and the most exquisite painting of fruit and flowers'. She found the mother-of-pearl, olive wood, japan china, jars of flowers and porcelain dishes had 'an enchanting effect'. She, like many others, was equally captivated by the gardens that lay behind yalis, with fountains and charming kiosks, covered in jasmine and honeysuckle.

The room in the yali projecting over the Bosphorus often has a grate in the floor, and you may see ladies amusing themselves by fishing in the waters below. A recent European visitor,

Giacomo Casanova, with a reputation with the ladies, enjoyed a night-time trip up the Bosphorus, and described his impression: 'As the moon glowed directly on the pool's water, we saw three nymphs who, at times swimming, at other times standing or sitting on the marble steps, offered themselves to our eyes in every imaginable way and in every manner of grace and voluptuousness.... You can imagine the ravages that this unique and ravishing spectacle must have incurred on my poor body.'

Another very popular venue is called Belgrade Village, three hours' ride north of the city and set within a forest. It was originally named after Serbian prisoners brought here by Suleyman the Magnificent. The forest is filled with magnificent trees: beech, oak, pine and elm. Over the years the sultans have built a number of kiosks here. The forest is a favourite spot for the European community during the summer months, taking walks or riding through the woods, heavy with the perfume of roses, lilies and narcissi. They play games, embark on shooting expeditions or try to trap birds. Lady Wortley Montagu loved the place when she spent some time there 30 years ago: 'I am in the middle of a wood, consisting chiefly of fruit trees, watered by a vast number of fountains famous for the excellency of their water, and divided into many shady walks upon short grass, that seems to me artificial but I am assured is the pure work of

The exquisite imperial palace of Sa'adabad and the gardens of Kagithane.

nature, within view of the Black Sea, from whence we perpetually enjoy the refreshment of cool breezes that makes us insensible of the heat of summer.' Christian women used to meet at a fountain near her house, where they would sing and dance, 'the beauty of the women exactly resembling the ideas of the ancient nymphs as they are given us by the representations of the poets and painters.'

The Sweet Waters of Europe, as the area at the top of the Golden Horn is known, is even more popular. During the last sultan Ahmed III's reign, the palace of Sa'adabad (meaning 'eternal happiness') and the gardens of Kagithane were a fantastic sight, adorned with fountains, cascades and wooden buildings painted in bright colours. Ahmed hated the formality of Topkapi, and spent as little time there as possible. If the rumours you will hear

are anything like the truth, this was a den of sybaritic vice, led by Ahmed's grand vizier and son-in-law Damad Ibrahim. Although Mahmud initially ordered the destruction of many imperial residences to disassociate himself from the previous regime, he has since restored the palatial grounds here to much of their original splendour. The palace itself has now gone, but many of the kiosks remain and, on a summer night, it seems that the whole of Istanbul has gathered here.

The area is filled with thousands of tents, with an array of performing acrobats, jugglers, acrobats, snake-charmers, sword-swallowers, fire-eaters, fortune-tellers and magicians doing tricks. The gardens are illuminated by lanterns, candles and torches, while the air is filled with the sound of music, and the sky is often illuminated by fireworks.

One of the most popular things to see in the gardens of Kagithane, and indeed all over the city, are theatrical shows and, in particular, *Karagoz* ('blackeye'). This a shadow play, with puppets made from the hides of camel or water buffalo. The shadows are projected onto a white muslin screen backlit by an oil lamp. The play itself has two main protagonists: Karagoz, an illiterate fellow, cynical, lustful and foul-mouthed, and Hacivat, an educated Turk, his speech flowered with poetical and literary allusions. Karagoz, with his peasant cunning, constantly outwits Hacivat, but his get-rich schemes always end in failure. The play allows full rein for Karagoz to indulge

A young man who has imbibed too much is deep in slumber.

in provocative jokes, obscene gestures and indecent innuendo, all of which are greeted with hoots of laughter by the audience. Other popular characters in the play are a drunkard, an eccentric dwarf, a half-wit, an opium addict and a number of flirtatious women.

When the play is over, you can wander through the gardens with their formal alleys of cypress trees and flower parterres, once the preserve of the upper classes but now open to all. Most are adorned with fountains and wooden platforms. They are meeting places for all classes, where people take walks and boat excursions, and enjoy swing rides. Men and women lounge on the grass, eating, drinking, smoking their water pipes and chatting, or, if the mood takes them, playing music and singing, while their children scamper around, riding swings and climbing trees. If you stroll through the more shaded areas, you will invariably come

across lovers engrossed with one another. Best not to look too closely; the older generation are shocked at what young lovers get up to. As one worried mother advised her daughter, none too subtly, 'Don't go to the fountain and get pregnant by Bekir Pasha. Pure, virginal and unsullied as you are, don't be deflowered.'

Not everyone is fortunate enough to enjoy this sybaritic lifestyle. You may notice common pedlars on the peripheries of gardens and parks, squatting on their heels, munching stale food, while their dogs snarl at one another among the heaps of rubbish. Their place of entertainment is known as Bitli ('lice-ridden') Kagithane. Some of these unfortunates take liberties and you need to watch out as they are expert at picking pockets. They have even been known to break into the sultan's gardens and steal his vegetables.

FESTIVALS

There seems to be no end of festivals. Apart from the religious ones (described in Chapter 8), the departure of the grand admiral for a tour of the Aegean is a cause for celebration, as is the grand vizier marching out at the head of his army for the spring campaign. These festivals give people a perfect chance to dress in all their finery and promenade through the streets. Shops and coffee houses stay open till dawn, their fronts festooned with flowers. You will know

when one begins when you see the lanterns strung between minarets lit up. In many squares four tall poles are erected, decorated with flowers, greenery and fruit, and covered by an awning. Bystanders love to soar up into the air on swings suspended from the poles.

Women enjoy watching these magnificent parades and are allocated specific viewing points. But many disregard these restrictions, revelling in the chance to get out and about. The authorities, anxious to maintain order, keep a close eye on their behaviour, with all sorts of regulations on what they can wear. It has been known for the sultan to order a festival to end prematurely because it is deemed to be too provocative.

Turks love a good parade almost as much as a festival. These parades are held by the military and by the guilds, often on religious feast days. Even more flamboyant are those celebrating the birth, circumcision or wedding of members of the sultan's family. They normally last four or five days, and are held on the hills above Topkapi Sarayi, or along the shores of the Golden Horn. The parades are accompanied by the din of incessant music; there is nothing that a Turk loves more than a band, playing with gusto on the rebeck, reed flute, zither and every type of drum.

One of the central features of most festivals is a chance for the Turks to express their love of sport. Wrestling matches, often lasting for hours, are very popular, although archery contests are not as common as they once were. You are more likely to see tricks of horsemanship, at which the Turks generally excel.

Many of the festivals are seasonal. 21 March is traditionally regarded as the beginning of spring, when the sultan sends gifts to his favourites. On 6 May, the feast of Hizir, Istanbul celebrates its role as naval capital of the Mediterranean. The great ships of the fleet, accompanied by a host of smaller craft, sail from the arsenal down the Golden Horn, to the sound of Turkish bands and the boom of cannons from forts on shore. At the Yali Kiosk, on the walls of Topkapi Sarayi, the captains are received by the sultan before setting off for a tour of the Aegean, where they receive rent from the various islands.

To celebrate the event the butchers in the city are given permission to slaughter lambs, which are a much sought-after delicacy. Locals head out to the country for the day to enjoy the holiday, and you will find the Sweet Waters of Europe and Asia covered in groups enjoying their picnics, the air filled with the delicious smell of pilau and dolma.

A PRINCE'S CIRCUMCISION

Many festivals are devoted to celebrating royal events: the accession of the sultan, the circumcision of his sons, or the wedding of his daughters. If you are lucky enough to witness one of these happy occasions, you will be alerted by the deafening noise of cannons; the Turks seem to use any pretext for firing these weapons, notably military victories or even when a ship sails past Topkapi Sarayi. As one disgruntled commentator noted, the din was such that 'the eyes and ears of the heavens became blind and deaf'.

The circumcision of the sultan's sons is treated as a very special event. Back in 1582 Murad III authorized that the festivities should last for an astonishing 50 days. And as recently as 1720, when four of Ahmed III's sons were circumcised and two of his nieces married, the celebrations lasted for 15 days. You may meet elderly locals whose eyes will light up when they describe the beauty of the firework displays and the illuminated models, some in fantastic shapes such as dragons, sailing down the Golden Horn past the sultan, who was watching from a raft. The most spectacular act was a carriage driven on a tightrope between the masts of ships anchored in the Bosphorus.

On land the streets were filled with acrobats, conjurors, tightrope-walkers, wrestlers and gypsies dancing, while thousands gathered to watch the popular shadow plays at night. The guilds, anxious to show their loyalty and not to be upstaged, produced elaborate *tableaux vivants* of their trades, displayed on carts or on a moving stage. Memorable examples were glass furnaces surrounded by workers

A crowd enjoys the sight of acrobats and buffoons during a festival.

Istanbul, the best place to go to is the Hippodrome, which tends to be the centre of the celebrations. All around you the major buildings will be lavishly decorated. There will be a festive air with tightrope-walkers will make their way along a rope stretched between the two obelisks.

One of the most extraordinary aspects of the occasion is the presentation to the sultan of gifts, including exotic animals such as giraffes and elephants. Most remarkable of all are the *nahils*, which are wooden poles symbolizing the young prince's phallus (the more intellectually minded like to stress how they actually symbolize birth, fertility and regeneration). They are decorated with fruit, flowers and sprouting foliage made of wax, created with loving care by the best craftsmen.

It has been known for locals, anxious to demonstrate their loyalty, to have their sons circumcised at the same time. This is partly due to the Muslim custom that when a rich man has his son circumcised, he may well feel generously disposed to pay for his poor neighbours to have the same honour done to their sons.

blowing glass, and wagons in which coffee beans were roasted, representing merchants of the flea market. As part of the celebrations the sultan authorized an all-day banquet where the poor and hungry could eat to their heart's content. Some 10,000 trays of rice coloured with saffron were consumed by the grateful populace.

If you have the opportunity to witness the scenes following a royal circumcision during your stay in

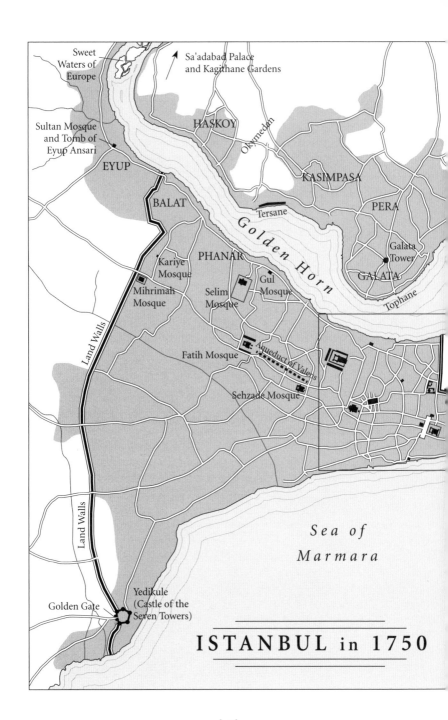

Sweet
Waters of
Europe

Sa'adabad Palace
and Kagithane Gardens

HASKOY

Okmeidan

Sultan Mosque
and Tomb of
Eyup Ansari

EYUP

KASIMPASA

PERA

BALAT

Tersane

G o l d e n   H o r n

Galata
Tower

Kariye
Mosque

PHANAR

GALATA

Mihrimah
Mosque

Selim
Mosque

Gul
Mosque

Tophane

Land Walls

Fatih Mosque

Aqueduct of Valens

Sehzade Mosque

Sea of
Marmara

Land Walls

Golden Gate

Yedikule
(Castle of the
Seven Towers)

ISTANBUL in 1750

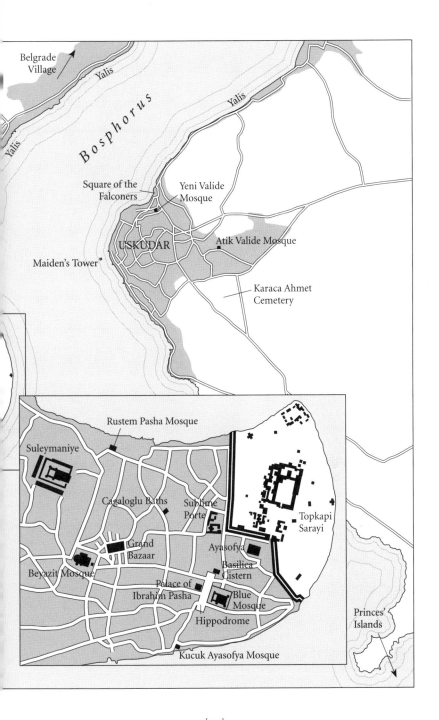

Belgrade
Village

Yalis

Yalis

B o s p h o r u s

Yalis

Yalis

Square of the
Falconers

Yeni Valide
Mosque

USKUDAR

Atik Valide Mosque

Maiden's Tower

Karaca Ahmet
Cemetery

Rustem Pasha Mosque

Suleymaniye

Cagaloglu Baths

Sublime
Porte

Topkapi
Sarayi

Grand
Bazaar

Ayasofya

Basilica
Cistern

Beyazit Mosque

Palace of
Ibrahim Pasha

Blue
Mosque

Hippodrome

Princes'
Islands

Kucuk Ayasofya Mosque

AUTHOR'S NOTE

The setting for this book is Istanbul in 1750. Although a few Grand Tourist quotes are slightly later, I have tried to make everything consistent with this date. I should particularly like to thank Philip Mansel, Norman Stone and Alexander de Groot for their advice, Ben Plumridge for his excellent editing, and all at Thames & Hudson for their help. I dedicate this book to my sons Nico and George, who have done their best to sleep through the early morning call of the muezzin and have attempted and failed to outwit the salesmen in the Grand Bazaar.

SOURCES OF QUOTATIONS

Numbers in brackets refer to the page upon which the quotation appears.

Arabic saying (quoted in Raphaela Lewis, *Everyday Life in Ottoman Turkey*, London, 1971) (69); Lord Baltimore, *A Tour to the East*, London, 1767 (17, 55, 68, 114); Ebru Boyar & Kate Fleet, *A Social History of Ottoman Istanbul*, Cambridge, 2010 (46, 119); Ogier Ghiselin de Busbecq, *The Turkish Letters*, trans. Edward Forster, Oxford, 1927 (9); *Giacomo Casanova: his life and memoirs*, trans. Arthur Machen, London, 1930 (132); Evliya Celebi, *In the Days of the Janissaries*, London, 1951 (99, 121); *The Travels of Sir John Chardin into Persia and the East-Indies*, London, 1686 (quoted in Philip Mansel, *Constantinople: City of the World's Desire*, London, 1995) (56); Lord Charlemont, *Travels in Greece and Turkey*, 1749 (ed. W.B. Stanford & E.J. Finopoulos, London, 1984) (27–28, 31, 62, 71, 113–14, 125); Contemporary account (quoted in Alan Palmer, *The Decline & Fall of the Ottoman Empire*, London, 1992) (70); Elizabeth, Baroness Craven, *A Journey Through the Crimea to Constantinople*, London, 1789 (116); Thomas Dallam, *Early Voyages and Travels in the Levant, The Diary of Thomas Dallam*, 1599–1600, ed. J. Theodore Bent, London, 1893 (104); Jean-Claude Flachat (quoted in Hilary Sumner-Boyd & John Freely, *Strolling Through Istanbul*, London & New York, 1987) (99–100, 104); Quoted in E.J.W. Gibb, *Ottoman Poems*, 1882 (53, 54); Guillaume-Joseph Grelot, *A Late Voyage to Constantinople*, 1683 (19); Peter Gyllius/Pierre Gilles, *The Antiquities of Constantinople*, trans. John Ball, New York, 1988 (6, 19, 82); Aaron Hill, *A Full and Just Account of the Present State of the Ottoman Empire*, 1710 (11, 26, 108, 117, 121); Justinian (quoted in William Joseph Grelot, *A Late Voyage to Constantinople*, trans. J. Philips, London, 1683) (77); Justinian quoted by Paul the Silentiary (quoted in Hilary Sumner-Boyd & John Freely, *Strolling Through Istanbul*, London & New York, 1987) (74); Quoted in Philip Mansel, *Constantinople: City of the World's Desire*, London, 1995 (59, 62, 112, 113, 115, 116); Lady Mary Wortley Montagu, *Turkish Embassy Letters*, London, 1993 (7–8, 13, 23, 24, 41, 42, 43, 46, 67, 132–33); Aubry de la Motraye, *Travels through Europe, Asia and into parts of Africa*, 1730 (12, 97); Sir James Porter, *Turkey: Its History and Progress*, London, 1854 (24, 46, 60, 66, 72); Comte d'Ollincan (quoted in J.A. Cuddon, *The Owl's Watchsong*, London, 1960) (112); George Sandys, *Sandys Travailes*, 1658 (quoted in Jason Goodwin, *Lords of the Horizons*, London, 1999) (113); Theodore Spandounes, *On the Origin of the Ottoman Emperors*, 1523 (trans. and ed. Donald M. Nicol, Cambridge, 1997) (32); Trad. saying (quoted in Lavendar Cassels, *The Struggle for the Ottoman Empire*, 1717–40, London, 1966, p.67) (20); Trad. Turkish love song (26); *Une Ambassade Francaise en Orient sous Louis XV – La Mission du Marquis de Villeneuve, 1728–41* (11–12).

SOURCES OF ILLUSTRATIONS

Key: a=above, b=below

akg-images 122
From Thomas Allom and Rev. Robert Walsh, *Constantinople and the Scenery of the Seven Churches of Asia Minor*, London, 1839 15, 41, 116
Michel Baudier, *Histoire Générale du Sérail et de la Cour du Grand Turc*, Paris, 1626 105
Bibliothèque Nationale, Paris 25
British Museum, London 56, 65
From Comte de Choiseul-Gouffier, *Voyage Pittoresque de la Grèce*, Paris, 1809 86
Collection Dagli Orti/Turkish and Islamic Art Museum, Istanbul/The Art Archive 1
From Guillaume Joseph Grelot, *Relation Nouvelle d'un Voyage de Constantinople*, Paris, 1680 9, 11, 18
From Jean Antoine Guer, *Moeurs et Usages des Turcs*, Paris, 1747 71
Sonia Halliday Photographs 78, 82, 103
Suna and Inan Kiraç Foundation Orientalist Painting Collection, Istanbul 2
From Le Hay and Charles de Ferriol, *Recueil de Cent Estampes Représentant Différentes Nations du Levant*, Paris, 1712 52, 61, 67, 108, 111, 118
From *Het Ellendigh Leven der Turcken*, I. Tongerloo, 1663 48b
Musée du Louvre, Paris 12
From Luigi Mayer, *Views in the Ottoman Dominions*, London, 1810 13
From Antoine Ignace Melling, *Voyage Pittoresque de Constantinople et Des Rives du Bosphore*, Paris, 1819 20, 100–01
From Aubry de la Motraye, *Travels Through Europe Asia and Into Part of Africa*, London, 1723–24 30, 106
Museo Correr, Venice 101
Trustees of the National Library of Scotland, Edinburgh 6–7
From N. de Nicolay, *Navigations et Peregrinations*, Lyon, 1568 23, 44, 45, 50, 54, 126
From Carsten Niebuhr, *Voyage en Arabie & en d'Autres Pays Circonvoisins*, Amsterdam, 1776 123
From Ignatius Mouradgea d'Ohsson, *Tableau Général de l'Empire Othoman…*, Paris, 1787–1824 133
From Julia Pardoe, *Beauties of the Bosphorus*, London, 1838 88
Ben Plumridge © Thames & Hudson Ltd 138–39
Private Collection 125
Private Collection/Archives Charmet/Bridgeman Art Library 8
Rijksmuseum, Amsterdam 68, 114
Courtesy Teylers Museum, Haarlem, The Netherlands 47, 53, 80–81, 130–31
Topkapi Museum, Istanbul 27, 42, 107, 119, 134, 137
Wellcome Library, London 31, 43, 48a, 98, 120

COLOUR PLATE SECTIONS
Archaeological Museum, Istanbul VII
Ashmolean Museum, Oxford VIII
British Library, London XV
British Museum, London VI
Collection Dagli Orti/Turkish and Islamic Art Museum, Istanbul/The Art Archive I
Gianni Dagli Orti/University Library, Istanbul/The Art Archive IV
Sonia Halliday Photographs X
Library of Congress, Washington, D.C., LC-USZC4-1186 III
Musée du Louvre, Paris XIII
Orientalist Museum, Doha II, XII, XIV
Rijksmuseum, Amsterdam V, IX, XI, XVII
Topkapi Museum, Istanbul XVI, XVIII

INDEX

First published in 2013 in hardcover in the United States of America
by Thames & Hudson Inc., 500 Fifth Avenue, New York, New York 10110

thamesandhudsonusa.com

Library of Congress Catalog Card Number 2012942997

ISBN 978-0-500-25193-5

Printed and bound in China by Toppan Leefung Printing Limited